W. J. Evelyn Ingram

Saint Crispin

And other quaint conceits and merry rhapsodies

W. J. Evelyn Ingram

Saint Crispin
And other quaint conceits and merry rhapsodies

ISBN/EAN: 9783337336240

Printed in Europe, USA, Canada, Australia, Japan

Cover: Foto ©Thomas Meinert / pixelio.de

More available books at **www.hansebooks.com**

SAINT CRISPIN

AND

Other Quaint Conceits

AND

MERRY RHAPSODIES.

BY

W. J. EVELYN INGRAM.

"Ne sutor ultra crepidam."

LONDON:
WILLIAM FREEMAN, 102, FLEET STREET.
1866.

The Author reserves the Right of Translation

CONTENTS.

	PAGE
SIR MAURICE; or, the Haunted Churchyard	1
THE ANGLER'S FATE: a Legend of Twickenham	11
THE REVELLER'S DREAM: a Legend of Brighton	15
YOUNG LAMBS TO SELL	31
A SEA-SIDE REVERIE	33
THE FLAT IRON: a Legend of St. Giles's	37
SAINT CRISPIN	43
WAIFS: a Legend of the Sea	97
THE BODY-SNATCHERS	119
THE LOST TESTIMONIAL: a Legend of Dundee	123
SAINT THAIS: a Legend of Thebes	127
THE MYRTLE AND LAUREL: a Treatife on Gardening	151
"SYMPATHY," and Where it may be found	153
LETHE. The Morning Thought of a Reveller	155
"THE EVERLASTING GOLD PEN."	157
"LOVE'S PUREST STAR"	159

	PAGE
"Meat *versus* Fish:" a Canonical Diſtinction	161
Reconciliation. The Blackſmith's Wife's Reply	165
The Wit and the Host: a Tale of the Ledger	167
"The Noisy Debate"	175
Untold Love	179
Ruth, the Gleaner	181
The "Stepping-stones:" a River Scene	183
The Devil Outwitted	191
Olla Podrida; or, Railway Jottings	195
The Baron and his Advisers	209

SIR MAURICE;

OR,

THE HAUNTED CHURCHYARD.

SIR MAURICE;

OR,

THE HAUNTED CHURCHYARD.

SIR Maurice was a knight of mighty arm,
    And had in Italy achieved renown;
No battles ever caufed his heart alarm;
As for a challenge—his reply a frown
    Of ftern defiance; ftill he felt a qualm
Whene'er he heard of ghofts or any fort of thing
He couldn't pink with fword, or with a bullet wing.

And this was all occafioned by thofe ftories
    So often told to people in their youth.
Of warfare he had heard, and all its glories
    Were grafted in his heart, becaufe their truth
Was patent to himfelf; but all about
The fupernatural he felt a doubt.

His nurse had often told him, when a boy,
   Of goblin, spectre, sorcerer, and sprite;
And, when he cried, she found the best alloy
   To talk of bogies, who took brats at night;
So that however brave might be his heart,
She curbed his mind, which was the better part.

He had been educated at a school
   Where moral courage was presumed a basis;
But superstition formed the fav'rite rule,
   And was in fact the very great oasis
On which his teachers fell to curb his tether,
For few could cope with such a bird of feather.

But early precepts never are forgotten;
   And in Italia's land, where they rely
On priestly miracles (altho' they're rotten),
   Yet the demand quite equals the supply;
He wonder'd how the Virgin could contrive
To wink the same when dead as if alive.

He saw the weeping image at Milan,
   "Saint Magdalen," who in her great emotion
Produced a stream of trickling tears, that ran
   To aid the unbelievers in devotion:

And he could not with truthfulness deny
He'd never seen the marble statue cry.*

Yet being told with all solemnity
  That such were facts he saw before his eyes,
How dare he doubt a priest's indemnity;
  On faith of some sort ev'ry one relies,
Such as the liquefaction of Saint Januarius,
The test of whose famed blood some think is most
  precarious.

He heard about the priests at Santiago,†
Who lay upon the women an embargo
For postage on all letters that are given
To priestly couriers who go up to heaven;

---

* The Florence correspondent of the *Indépendance Belge* says that a singular discovery has been made in a church in one of the faubourgs of Milan. A statue of Saint Magdalen, which has been long famous for weeping in the presence of unbelievers, was recently moved in order to facilitate repairs in the church. It was found that the statue contained an arrangement for boiling water, the steam from which passing into the head, was there condensed, and making its way by a couple of pipes to the eyes, trickled down the cheeks of the image: so the wonderful miracle was performed.

† In the accounts of the destruction by fire of the Cathedral at Santiago, when some 2000 females were burnt, it was mentioned that the priests had erected a letter-box for women

For when the ladies' sins require purging,
They then indite a letter to the Virgin.

But what her answers were to their petition,
　　Or if the priests had forged her autograph,
Were points by far too moot for his cognition;
　　Their conduct at the fiery cenotaph
Was like Nero's, who, tender feelings spurning,
Could play the fiddle while the place was burning.

And sundry strange conceptions that he saw,
　　Descended like an heirloom we inherit;
Tho' here and there he might detect a flaw,
　　Still on the whole it acted on his spirit,
And gave to all he couldn't understand
A certain awe, which held him in command.

Beside the Abbey where the yew tree blows,
　　Obtaining life distilled from dead men's bones,
There by its side the weeping willow grows,
　　Bending its languid leaves upon the stones—

---

to send petitions to the Virgin. By the priests' persistence in closing the door of the sacristy to enable them to remove the valuables of the church—and themselves—in safety, they were the cause of preventing hundreds escaping from the dreadful immolation.

"Death's monuments"— where man in vain
    records
The laſt frail trace humanity affords.

Rumour a tale about that yard had ſpread,
    That in the night a ghoſt walked o'er the dead;
And ſome who had been known to paſs alone
    Beſide the charnel-houſe, had heard a groan,
In which direction, by the moon's pale light,
With horror they beheld the awful ſight.

The tale got wind among the population
    About the time the knight arrived at home;
It was a theme of gen'ral conſternation,
    And after dark ſcarce any one would roam
Within the precincts of a ſpot ſo dread,
Where walked the reſtleſs and unholy dead.

A poor old faithful widow, who had laid
Her huſband in his grave, was ne'er afraid
Of ghoſts. In tribulation of the mind
She thought a calm in ſolitude to find;
And ev'ry night went forth in grief to mourn,
Beſide the ſhadow of his hallowed urn.

And there was feasting in an ancient hall,
    The wassail cup had made each heart rejoice,
While none could dream dark danger could appal
    Each noisy guest (if one might judge by voice).
But in the midst of all their revelry
The conversation turned on devilry,

And then on spirits which return'd to earth—
    Revisiting the glimpses of the night—
When far less loud became the roist'ring mirth,
    Or, plainly speaking, disappeared in fright;
For manly roaring to soft whispers sunk,
And no more merry toasts that night were drunk.

Then up arose (fresh from the battle-field)
    Sir Maurice—he whose valour ne'er did fail—
And cried, "Ye knights! a blot upon the shield
.   "Of each who at old women's stories quail!
"Go to the churchyard, if you're brave and true."
The answer was, "Sir Maurice, pray will you?"

Thus called upon—altho' to him distasteful,
    And tho' in secret not a little daunted—
He thought refusal would appear disgraceful
    By those whose courage he had just now taunted.

He knew " Neceſſitas non habet leges,"
But this beat all his battles and his ſieges.

Thus being challenged, he perforce conſented.
    True to his word he ſought the drear abode
(Tho' ſorely his pot-valour he repented),
    And entered where the troubled ſpirit ſtrode ;
Yet was not ſpirit in that haunted ground
So troubled as his own—as now he found.

Till now he ne'er had made a recantation
    Of his belief in either ſprite or ghoſt,
And ſtraightway he commenced his incantation,
    One part in fear, and one in noiſy boaſt ;
For well he knew it would not do to lag,
Tho' when he held the beaker he could brag.

" If there be any who have paſſ'd Death's portal,
    " Or who upon his late life ſadly ponders,
" I call upon that moſt unhappy mortal,
    " Or rather ſpirit who in ſpace now wanders,
" Whether it be in England, Spain, or France, ſir,
" This moment I demand to have an anſwer."

In pauſing for reply, he thought he heard
    A curious ſort of noiſe in his proximity;
His blood felt chilled, and yet he never ſtirred
    (It was the ruſtling of the widow's dimity);
But hearing nothing more he thought he needed
More energy, and thus again proceeded:

"Report aſſerts that from ſome awful cauſe
    "Thou wand'reſt here, for ſome affirm they've
        ſeen thee.
"Say why thou violateſt nature's laws?
    "For not a ſhadow of thy ſhade ſhall ſcreen
        thee;
"My voice is huſky, yet I've no horſe laugh,
"Nor, like my horſe, do I indulge in 'chaff.'

"Tell me the truth while I am ſtanding by—
    "You'll find, by Jove, that I'll allow no quarter;
"And if you do not inſtantly comply,
    "Upon your tombſtones I'll commence a
        ſlaughter.
"With my moſt famed of ſwords an inſult you
    ſhould ſettle:
"If you've the ſpirit of a ghoſt, come, ſhow your
    mettle!"

The frail and trembling widow in her sorrow
    Had heard these threats and very dark menaces,
And luckily it was not near the morrow,
    Whose rosy light had shown his vile grimaces;
While she, poor soul, was at the theological,
His mind was working at the diabolical.

These horrid imprecations 'midst the gloom
    Aroused the silent figure from the grave,
And with a shriek she fainted on the tomb;
    Off bolted he, his craven self to save—
The only reveller who dared to roast
His friends about existence in a ghost.

Had he possessed the courage that he vaunted,
    And stayed, he would have seen that his affright
Was not caused by the churchyard being haunted,
    But would have found, to his intense delight,
Instead of meeting with a ghost or elf,
'Twas one almost as frightened as himself.

He staggered homewards looking like a spectre,
    With such a frenzied brain as terror warps;
He found the widow such a stern reflector,
    That in a week he was himself a corpse.

And thus Sir Maurice, now as cold as ſtone,
By ſeeking for a ghoſt gave up his own.

Moral.

Written as an Epitaph for Sir Maurice' Cenotaph.

Imagination paints fictitious things,
    And out of fancy oft a goblin ſprings;
No churchyard has the power to diſcloſe
    Such horrors as poor timid hearts ſuppoſe.
The germ of ev'ry ghoſt in ſuperſtition lies—
Created in the brain, which ignorance ſupplies.

THE ANGLER'S FATE.

A LEGEND OF TWICKENHAM.

ROBERT Jones one morning very
    Early took a fishing wherry,
      Not at Wapping Old Stairs,
      Where your Molly declares
Her love will be true till she dies,
    But at Twickenham Ait,
    Where the connoisseurs state
The eels taste so nice in the pies.

    You never could halt on
      A man who had studied
    Piscatorial Walton,
      Or a brain half so flooded
With all the enticements of ground-bait or fly,
To hook out a fish wheresoever he'd lie.

His mind did inherit
The famed Izaak's spirit;
His walls were well embellish'd by
Stuffed victims of the treach'rous fly,
All splendid specimens of fish
To gratify an angler's wish,
The trophies of his former sport,
Alas! this fatal day cut short.

While Bob was peering from the boat
Watching the bobbing of his float,
The 'thwart gave way, and back he fell,
Soused like a pickled mack-e-rel.
Although his muscles were alive,
He could not swim, but he could dive;
His heel stuck in the mud so tight,
Much to the other eels' delight;
And thus poor Jones, once an Oxonian,
Died—by becoming a Waltonian.

It is reported since that day
The eels a finer taste display;
But why?—"The Reason Why" don't say:
Perhaps from feelings of dismay;

And we've been told it ill became us
To spoil the sale of pies so famous.
We recommend " Enquire Within "—
The work to answer everything—
And shut your ears, and do not see
The link of Jones' cataftrophe.
But I moft diligently sought
The Twickenham Regiftrar's report,
And find that Jones was not interr'd;
By which 'tis eafily inferr'd,
And very greatly to be dreaded,
His corpfe has only been imbedded;
That is, the refidue of bone—
The Lord knows where the flesh has gone.

THE
REVELLER'S DREAM.

A LEGEND OF BRIGHTON.

THE REVELLER'S DREAM.

A LEGEND OF BRIGHTON.

PETER Carew, a captain in the Lancers,
   Was always thought a paragon of
     dancers;
  In Scotch or Irish reels
  He'd twist and twirl his heels,
  No bee with pin
  Stuck through his skin
Could turn with such velocity:
  Not one in a million
  Could dance a cotillon
Like this young famed precocity.
   He'd never step false
   When dancing a waltz,
   But would spin like a top
   Until ready to drop;

For he felt the intenſity
Of the twirling propenſity.
　　Nor did he e'er forget
　　Politeneſs in a minuet;
　　Like the ſaid bee he'd pirouette,
And make a ſalaam, when he look'd in the face full
Of his partner, madam, who thought it moſt graceful.

This Captain Carew was an exquiſite ſwell,
And owned the affections of many a belle;
　　Of muſic he'd talk
　　While dancing a polk;
'Twould have opened the eyes of poor blind Beliſarius
To ſee him and Miſs Glibly perform the cellarius;
And Miſs G. would in turn play upon the piano,
While he danced with another the varſoviana.
Baron Nathan aſſerts of illuſtrious dancers,
That Peter invented the "ſet" called the "Lancers."
The ladies, thoſe darling and lovely philoſophers,
Declared him to be the moſt charming of officers;
In giving a toaſt or breathing a ſentiment,
Not one was like him in the whole of the regiment.

THE REVELLER'S DREAM.

But I'm forry to fay
That this captain fo gay,
In addition to dancing
Was alfo advancing
In numerous purfuits
Which produced evil fruits.
It's a fecret worth knowing—
Tho' I'm not fond of "blowing"
The trumpet belonging to fame—
But it has been reported
That the captain reforted
To the " bottle "—I think that's the name.

And it's alfo related that fcarce one or two
Could sit up and drink, like young Peter Carew,
Without feeling dizzy and faying things rude—
A ftate beft defcribed by a word they call "fcrewed."

One night, after doing a dance and a booze,
He went home to bed like a lonely recluse,
And had juft fallen off in a foft happy fnooze,
When the wine he'd been drinking and couldn't refufe
Concocted a "dream" of the "horrible blues."

A ſtrange ſort of feeling came into his noddle:
Tho' ſtill half aſleep, he thought he muſt toddle
In any direction but where he was lying;
For all ſorts of goblins came peeping and prying
With horrible grins, and great ſaucer eyes,
And carbuncle noſes, which drinking ſupplies.
Theſe hideous companions kept quietly eyeing
Poor Peter Carew in his unhappy fix,
Whoſe brain ſeemed a deluge of Lethe or Styx:
  No flying-fiſh, ſkimming
   The water ſo bright,
  Could have a "head ſwimming"
   Like Peter that night.

But the mind, ever active on one thing or other,
Made him think himſelf "Fiſh," and the Devil his brother.
It's ſtrange the excitement a frenzied brain feels
When worked up with wine; and the nightmare reveals
"The identical perſon" he thought his relation,
And thus, in his "Dream," he began the oration:
  "O Devil! to thee
  "For ſuccour I flee;
"State, ſtate but thy terms, to all I'll agree;

" Releafe me at once, and give me fome quarter;
" If I'm really a fifh—' I'm a fifh out of water!'
" Give, give me, dear Devil, the power to lave
" 'Neath the waters fo pure, 'neath the bright briny wave;
  " For, tho' glorious the earth,
  " Where I firft derived birth,
" Since fome vile transformation has made me a 'Fifh,'
  " The earth and the air,
  " However fo fair,
" Are ufelefs to me and no longer my wifh."

He imagined the Devil was ftanding before
Him, and granting him all he could wifh to implore;
Had he treated him harfhly he perhaps might have fainted,
But found "he was not quite fo black as he's painted."
  Said the Devil—" I grant
  " The water you want;
" I think you'll enlighten at fome future day
" The remnant that's left of humanity's clay;
" I've watched you for long, and I find you difplay

" A talent superior to most in their revels,
" And a candidate likely to have the 'blue devils.'
" You once were a man, but I've made you a 'Triton,'
" You're now in the depths of the ocean, off
    Brighton;
" At present you rest on a nice sandy pillow,
" Arrived by the 'header' you took through the
    billow;
    " You are near my 'estate,'
      " I have granted the boon;
    " Be resigned to your fate,
      " I will call again soon."

    Become an aquatic,
    He felt quite ecstatic,
    Tho', much like an eel,
    At times he would feel
    A certain intensity
    We'll call a propensity,
That when of the ocean he didn't feel fond,
    He'd never despond,
But migrate, 'like a bird,' to another fish-pond.*

---

  * In a recent work " On the Pike," by Mr. Pennell, it is

THE REVELLER'S DREAM.

   It's a curious affair
   How the eels can get there,
And well worth a queſtion or two I would aſk,
For it ſeemeth to be a moſt difficult taſk.
   Firſt determine their breed—
   For I feel much in need
   Of ſome clever authority—
   I would call a majority
   Of practical men,
   Who could ſay there and then
   How theſe creatures meander,
   Like any old gander,
   From one pond to another
   Without any bother;
And a friend has aſſerted that no one can prove
An iota or word of their ſerpentine love:
   He, being maſonic,
   Thinks it may be platonic.

But juſt as he'd think of the ſubject no longer,
He floated—good gracious!—againſt a large conger;

---

aſſerted that the pike has alſo the power of taking the "overland route" from one pond to another, and has been caught in the act of doing ſo.

There's one confolation, when he was a man
'Twas not a bad difh—let them eat it who can.
   If you meet with a bull,
    Tho' you've often been full
  Of beef, yet it's one thing to have it
    By way of a bake,
    Or elfe a rump fteak,
  If your appetite happens to crave it;
And having the bull or the conger well frizzled
Is all very nice; but I think you'd have mizzled,
If in *propriâ perfonâ* either one fhould attack you,
Unlefs at your heels you'd the Devil to back you.
But the conger fhied off, though I can't tell the
  reafon,
Unlefs fuch an aquamarine out of feafon
    As he might appear,
    Caufed the " long-back " fome fear;
But certain it is, it put Peter in mind
  That no fort of ill-life that any poor cur fpent
Could equal the dread of all dreads he would find,
  If ever he floated againft the " fea-ferpent."
    He heard a poor fkate
    Lamenting her fate,
    And fadly relate

That her husband, she heard, was given to trailing
After a creature they call a Miss Grayling;
And another vile wretch—a common An-chovy—
Kept sneaking about to entrap her "old covey."

Had famed Justice Wilde been a child of the ocean,
Amongst all the fish there'd have been a commotion;
For Peter Carew felt himself much astonished
To find that "loose fish" should indeed be admonished,
And also to see that a charm or love philter
Can act on a spawner as well as a milter.

  It's folly to think,
  Howe'er we may wink,
  That fish of the sea
  Cannot equally see
As well as ourselves any cool dereliction,
  Or feel the affliction
  Of fondest affection
So often bestowed in another direction.

If the said Justice Wilde, with his usual precision,
Would only pop down and just give his decision,

I'm certain the fiſh would be dancing with glee;
    For in fits of dejection
    They'd feel no objection
To tickle each other with law coſts and fee.

    He fancied he ſaw
    A lobſter and crab
    Diſputing while picking
    A poor little dab;
    The ſtrife ran ſo ſore
    They both got a licking
(The combat was almoſt "a draw");
    But the crab did aſpire,
    In the heat of his ire,
To tear from the lobſter a claw,
    Which he ſtuck to, and bore
Triumphantly off with the greateſt *éclat*.*

He ſaw the old fiſh, like mortals on earth
When they grew up in age, got well up in girth;
And tho' many a ſtorm aroſe on the ocean,
'Twas as quiet below as moſt folks at devotion.

---

* Walker pronounces it e-*klaw*; I therefore take him as a convenient authority for the rhyme.

'Twas ſtrange he eſcaped from the jaws of a
    ſhark;
        And a "bottle-noſe whale"
        With a flap of his tail
        Threw Peter into a quandary;
But being aſleep he was ſafe in the dark,
    Tho' prying "the realms of fairy."*

        He ſaw oyſters and prawns,
        Sword-fiſh, with long horns,
        With herrings and codfiſh,
        And ſome that looked "odd fiſh;"
        John O'Dories—good ſtuff—
        Whales well up in puff,
        "Periwinkle and ſhrimp,"
        With the poor ſkate they crimp,
        And plenty of ſalmon—
        Tho' fiſhmongers gammon
        To keep up the price
        Becauſe it's ſo nice;
But I cannot name all of the nautical crew
Which paſſed in his ſight like "a ſplendid review."

* "Don Juan."

There's one thing he miffed—'twould have been
    a great treat
To fee " Father Neptune " enthroned on his feat,
With his horfes, and alfo his trident in hand,
And the fair " Amphitrite," his Queen, in com-
    mand ;
But from what Peter heard, he had ftarted away
On a " tour of infpection " to Botany Bay.

What he moftly approved of, and faw well
    difplayed,
Was the figure and face of a lovely mermaid,
As fhe fat in a cavern of cryftal and coral
Surrounded by fea-weeds, aquatic and floral.
Had her eyes fhone on earth like the famed Bafilifk,
He'd have run, he'd have fwum, and encounter'd
    the rifk :
Galvani and Volta could not fhoot a battery
Of love as he would do—without any flattery.

    I think we'll drop the curtain now,
    For fear a frown would not allow;
    But—Query : How is Peter's brow?
    He got as drunk as " David's fow."

Lift, my good friends, my true upholders,
He shook the " Old Man " from his shoulders.*
In the morn, when the fumes of the wine had abated,
He awoke from his "horrible dream" quite elated,
Altho' he imagined he'd been all the night
Subdued by the ocean, and in a wet plight;
      He felt no regret
      To feel himself dry,
      And thought " heavy wet "
      The best thing to try.

---

* " Arabian Nights—Sinbad."

YOUNG LAMBS TO SELL.

IN the heyday of youth, when I was a boy,
I ne'er ſhall forget how my heart beat with joy,
When my deareſt Aunt Jenny
From her purſe took a penny,
And ſaid—" You ſhall have a moſt innocent toy;"

For mind and obſerve,
Her auricular nerve
Caught loud as it fell
That old-faſhioned knell
Of " Young lambs to ſell!
" If I'd as much money as I could tell," &c.

The toy having bought,
My dear aunt I ſought.

When with kifs and carefs
She exclaimed—" Heaven blefs
" And make you, dear Tommy, a good little child,
" Like the lamb in its manners, fo meek and fo
  " mild ;
" May you ne'er go aftray, or ever turn wild."

Such were the dreams of my youth ;
But fince I've grown up, forsooth !
I find my aunt told an untruth.

Whene'er in the meadows by chance you are
  rambling,
You'll find that young lambs are devoted to
  "gamb'ling ; "
"*They lay* on the turf," and with "blacklegs"
  affociate !
Could you ever fpeak worfe of any young
  profligate ?
Yet fuch is the life of an innocent lamb,
And when mamma dies "he is not worth a dam."

A SEA-SIDE REVERIE.

UPON the shore where breakers roll,
   Fulfilling their eternal goal,
   A female stood with accents mute,
As if borne down with grief acute.
She from her warm and humble bed—
Though by her side another slept—
With step most stealthily had crept,
To come that night in fear and dread;
For as she ran towards the tide,
She seemed intent on suicide.
The vital streams within her breast,
Like the rough sea, could gain no rest:
She gazed most eager and intent on
The sea, to find the drift 'twas bent on;
For she'd a doubt upon her mind,
To her of a distressing kind.

Her anxious heart would feel elate,
Inſtead of feeling now diſtreſſed,
Should in the night the ſtorm abate—
Her fondeſt wiſhes would be bleſſed;
But now the ſurge appeared appalling—
"A fiſherman" her huſband's calling.

The Lady Goldpurſe had come down
To ruſticate in their ſmall village;
'Twas much too little for a town,
And more for paſturage than tillage.
There ſhe poſſeſſed a country ſeat,
With lawns and plants arranged ſo neat;
And came before the leaves got ſear,
At that delightful time of year
When nature ſmells divinely ſweet.

The Lady Goldpurſe liked a reliſh,
Her breakfaſt-table to embelliſh;
And all the niceties in ſeaſon
She had—of courſe, in common reaſon.
Tho' in the winter ſhe liked fawns,
In ſummer ſhe indulged in prawns;
And for the firſt and fineſt diſh
Of this moſt ſweet cruſtaceous fiſh,

She always gave a handfome prize,
Combining quality with fize.

This kept the fifhwife all night waking,
Not for her hufband's fafety quaking;
For he was fnug at home and fnoring,
Unmindful of the billows roaring,
While fhe was wifhing in the early morn,
The fea fo fmooth that he might go to " prawn."
That's why that female ftood aghaft at night,
Watching the fea with fuch intenfe affright.

THE FLAT IRON.

A LEGEND OF ST. GILES'S.

Dedicated to My Uncle.

THERE are peculiar ways of doing trade,
    And out of trade we know that money's made;
Like lively maggots crawling in a bowl,
We live upon each other heart and foul.
But what the abſtract of ſuch ſweets may be
Requires judgment and great nicety;
For few with capital know where to fix
Their habitation, ere they "cut their ſticks,"
Finding the thing don't anſwer; then another
Pays for "goodwill" without the ſlighteſt bother,
Thinking the trade's eſtabliſhed; and what then?
Before a year has paſſed he cries—"Amen!"

Yet some can live where others would be starving,
By what is called the happy knack of carving.
I'll try if I can illustrate a point,
By one whose brain was not thought out of joint.

A man whose "sign" was "two to one"—
"Three golden balls," bright like the sun—
Was well aware of one great fact,
That out of little much is done,
And if you multiply the act,
Into a large amount 'twill run.
Among the customers who came
To pledge their trifles at his shop,
Was one poor soul—one Betty Tame—
Who on the Saturday would pop
An old "Flat Iron," and the same
She always took again from pawn
The first thing on the Monday morn.

Now "Spout" considered in himself,
" This is the way to make the pelf—
" A monthly interest for a day
" Must be the sort of thing to pay;

" And every week, too, a new ticket—
" A halfpenny more—that's how I nick it."

So things went on, until of late
She came not to oppignorate.
"Spout" thought of her with great regret,
Until one day he met old Bet,
And ſtepping up to her moſt eager—
Juſt as he was, an old intriguer—
Exclaimed, "God bleſs me! how d'ye do?
" Who would have thought of ſeeing you!
" I've often wondered what has been
" The reaſon I have never ſeen
" You at my ſhop of late ; but ſtill,
" I hope that you have not been ill,
" Although you look a little pale.
" What ſay you, Betty, to ſome ale?
" 'Twill cheer your heart and warm your blood,
" And p'rhaps do you 'a world of good.'"

" Oh! Sir—indeed, the truth to tell,
" I'd call as I have done for years,
" But that an accident befell—
(Here Betty's eyes were dimmed with tears)—

"The poor 'Flat Iron,' which I had
"So many years, at laſt got bad,
"And—true a word as e'er I ſpoke—
"Fell from my careleſs hand—and broke.'

"Oh! Betty, don't let that cauſe ſorrow,
"But come into my ſhop to-morrow,
"And, out of old acquaintance' ſake,
"With pleaſure from my ſtock I'll take
"An iron that is ſpick-ſpan new,
"And as an off'ring make to you."

They parted with a mutual feeling,
Old "Covetous" his thoughts concealing,
And Betty with a grateful heart
To think ſhe'd got another ſtart.

As uſe becomes a ſecond nature,
So fared it with the poor old creature;
The ſame old game ſhe uſed to play
Commenced again next Saturday.
From then, and ever after that,
The iron, which they name "The Flat,"
Produced its value o'er and o'er,
Enough to buy a bumping ſcore.

Moral.

Lay well your bait to catch the fiſh,
As old "Spout" did, to gain his wiſh;
And thus you'll find that a falſe kindneſs
Is often ſwallowed up in blindneſs.

SAINT CRISPIN.

THE

TITULAR SAINT OF SHOEMAKERS

SAINT CRISPIN.

THE TITULAR SAINT OF SHOEMAKERS.

'VE heard of a thread—" the thread of a theme,"
And alfo of thread they ufe in a feam;
But one's for a poet, the next for a tailor,
And " long yarn's " the ufual thread of a failor.
Ariadne the fair, by the clue of a thread,
From the Lab'rinth her Thefeus moft cunningly led.*
The daughters of Nox† fpin the thread of our life;
And a god once fpun thread for the fake of a wife.‡
Penelope's web was a thready difplay,
Undoing at night what fhe did in the day:
She kept all her troublefome fuitors at bay.

---

* Minotaur.   † The Fates.   ‡ Omphale.

But my proper thread a "Wax-end" shall be,
As more in confistence with "cobblery."
So spin away now, my merry "Wax-end,"
In an ambling pace my wishes befriend;
If anything knotty should run in the vein,
Be careful, and don't let's entangle the skein.

Bibo Bibere mended shoes,
His pious wife attended pews,
To sweep, to clean, and make them tidy,
Ready for Sunday or for Friday,
And singing-days when they rehearse,
But Friday suits me in the verse.
  Whene'er you write a word,
   No matter how you time it,
  To alter looks absurd,
   As if you couldn't rhyme it.

  While the priest was preaching at church,
Where sinners are taught the things they should do,
And especially those they ought to eschew,
  Bibo upon his usual perch,
   Tho' not given to pray
   At that time of day,
Was mending the "soles" of a different crew.

Of jobs on hand he always had
A specimen of good and bad,
And when folks brought a well-worn shoe
He'd see how much there was to do;
His time and price would then accord;
But if he found the cash they'd hoard,
And say they couldn't much afford,
He didn't say he wouldn't do it:
Instead of stitching he would glue it;
And by example let them find
It's better not a snob to grind.

    His wife was a Catholic woman;
      She had also a heavenly nose;
        But as far as that goes,
       You're not led to suppose
   Her nose was by any means Roman;
Its heavenly tendency turned to the skies—
        Retroussé,
     As the French would say—
And divided a pair of lovely blue eyes.
Her complexion was fair, with nut-brown hair,
And pearly teeth, with which few could compare;

Such a sweet pretty mouth, with a curl to the lip,
Which greatly subdued the nose at the tip.

Her figure was neither short nor tall,
But a medium proportion between the two—
Its gen'ral contour handsome you'd call—
With a very small foot, and on it a shoe,
With half a glance there could be no mistake
But that it was one of Bibo's "best make."

There's a lott'ry in life in choosing a wife,
Midst the chances and ways of the doing;
    For you'll find, tho' you're rife,
    There may yet be some strife
In the method of cooing and wooing;
For men are like cherries, the finest and best
Are always henpecked—no one cares for the
    rest.
    In searching for bliss
    May you meet with a Miss—
—fortune—divided in half like my lines
(Forgive me for sev'ring the two I suggest):
In the eyes of the world it most surely opines
A much better chance if you wish to be blest;

For when you've a Mifs with fortune attached,
" Golden dreams "—" golden eggs "—are fure to
    be hatched.

When preffed for a rhyme, it's a good way by
    " fplit—
—ting hairs "—or p'rhaps words, for it feems it's
    admit—
—ted—" poetical targets"—the bull's-eye to hit,
Like a bul-let it flies with abundance of wit.

" Variety is charming," but our wives
    Don't feem to entertain the fame opinion ;
They rather think that fhe who beft contrives
    Should o'er the houfehold hold the great
        dominion ;
And by a fond perfuafion, not by force,
Prove " the grey mare to be the better horfe."

Or read us curtain lectures when we ftand
    Befide the fanctity of her bed-poft,
Expecting queftions anfwered quite off-hand,
    While we're perfonifying " Pepper's ghoft ; "
And whilft our purfes have the power to flow,
Declare that " money makes the mare to go."

E

If I could bait my pen
    As fifhermen do hooks,
Perchance there might be men
    Who'd patronife my books;
And tho' my lines may be
    Compofed of diff'rent thread,
I only hope to fee
    Their chance of being read.
However, on I go,
    Regardlefs as to that—
I'm not the firft below
    Who's given out the "fprat,"
Without at all inferring
    That I fhall "catch the herring."

I know not if the world has grown fedate,
And entered into a more ferious ftate;
But fadly, folemnly do I relate,
That rifibility is out of date.

Unlefs by chance we meet a giggling maid,
The elder ones appear demure and ftaid;
And fome don't laugh becaufe their teeth are faid
To be imperfect when they are difplayed.

But "laughter" certainly did once abound;
However flight the thought on which 'twas ground,
Its merry, happy peals, would oft refound,
Whene'er fome fterling wit or jeft was found.

In thefe hard days of thought and enterprife,
Each one upon his energy relies,
And half the pleafures of the world denies—
With fome from need, others to aggrandize.

But in the prefent day and prefent tenfe,
Hilarity is not thought common fenfe;
To laugh aloud is reckoned an offence,
And favours much of verdant innocence.

"Laugh and grow fat" was faid to parties thin;
"A jolly laugh," and not a puny grin,
To curb the ebullition felt within;
But now 'tis only "Let thofe laugh that win."

Obefity's not pleafant, and one "Banting"
Compofed a work, upon that theme defcanting,
To put an end to all afthmatic panting,
And modify a weafy actor's ranting.

His screws upon the feelings quite confound one:
A hearty " Ha! ha!" really would astound one.
Take any lengthy march, and I'll be bound one
Has scarce been met that felt inclined to sound one.

I'm delighted to find the world's getting better:
Altho' I'd give vent, still I feel there's a fetter
To curb every thought that would " kick over traces."
" I'll sing humble pie," for fear that some faces
Might draw a " long mug " with a " nut-cracker chin,"
As they purse up their mouth, and exclaim, " Oh! what sin,"
    That in these days of grace
    Any one should misplace
A word with a doubt, which would make a soul ponder,
And find, after all, it is *double entendre*.

    Had the great Rabelais
    Been alive at this day,
He'd have found himself muzzled and little to say;

Like the poor canine tribe, he'd have found a prevention
Put over his caput to stop the intention.
O Lights of the Past! where is Swift? where is Sterne?
And the "great Alexander"?—I mean little Pope:
Tho' your body was crooked your mind had a scope,
    That, while language shall last,
    You can ne'er be o'ercast,
But your eloquence radiant eternally burn;
But if your "shade" should meet me—say to-night—
I'd tell you one thing—which was not polite—
  For which you're blamed, and I'll not take your part;
But 'tis reported you did falsely say,
To trusting husbands' and their wives' dismay,
    "That ev'ry woman is a rake at heart;"
    And then that greater libel you let fall—
    "Most women have no characters at all."

Until we meet the subject must remain
For ev'ry man and wife to quibble over;
And you of course the secret will retain,
Since you're the only man who could discover
This "bitter pill" for ev'ry faithful lover.

But as your mind sarcastically waged,
We cannot wonder that sometimes, enraged,
You'd "spit your spite" upon "the weaker vessel,"
And form a "Tartar" for poor man to wrestle—
An unexpected one for him to "catch"—
And prove a "lord of the creation's" match.
But as you probably were never wed,
I think 'twas spleen by which your brain was led,
To raise up doubts upon our marriage beds,
And set both men and wives at "loggerheads."

Caseley has studied "The Rape of the Lock,"
And help'd himself well to the jeweller's stock;
But his skill would have been on the wrong "side of Jordan,"
If the safe had been made by the famed Samson Mordan.
Talking of Samson recalls to my mind
A chapter I fancy in Judges you'll find,
Where Delilah (whose conduct all modesty shocks),
Found Samson's "safeguard" was contained in his "locks."
This is a fact I've derived from the Bible,
And inserting it here gives no action for libel.

Bibo, 'twas reported, was "up to fnuff,"
But not for his nofe—he preferred a puff
Of tafty tobacco by way of a fmoke;
He could fing a good fong, and crack a good joke,
And a fly bit of fun at his neighbours poke.
Sometimes, irafcible, he'd in a ftorm
Of indignation fpeak about the "Rights
"Of Man," and then about a "Great Reform"
Some people look upon as only blights;
But "Univerfal Suffrage" will fome day
Proclaim the "Age of Reafon" bears the fway.

 If any of them "came it ftrong,"
 Or drew "the bow that's chriftened long,"
 To act on his credulity;
 It always was a rule that he
  Would never fay they lied;
 But put his thumb unto his nofe,
 If in his mind a doubt arofe,
  And fpread his fingers wide.
  To put your thumb unto your nofe,
   And then fuppofe

Your little finger an extender,
    Merely means—" To take a fight "—
" Over the left "—" Over the bender "—
    Nearly fynonymous, or quite,
  Tranflated in a vulgar light;
    Tho' not uncivil
An act—I've as much right to handle too
As any one—" to hold the candle to
    Old Nick, the Devil."

Of beer he ne'er cried " *Jam fatis* "*—enough,
    Or the other oration,
    Or rather quotation,
    When he took a potation—
I mean what the doctors call " *quantum fuff.*"
    I'm writing now of beer,
      Tho' Horace wrote of fnow;
    But mine's the better cheer—
    At leaft I'm thinking fo.

By Horace and fnow I will not be outdone;
But open my portholes and run out a gun,
Or elfe have a tilt, for the fake of mere fun.

---

* Horace, Ode 2, vol. i.

Presto! I've got it in a trice;
Instead of snow, I'll take to ice—
In summer-time it's very nice.
So listen to a friend's advice—
In fact you'd better note it
Precisely as I quote it:—
When thirst is great and appetite tiny,
Don't drink hot grog—try "*frigidum sine.*"

'Twas all Greek to him about Sardanapalus,
Yet he ran like a man, "flap bang," to an alehouse.
  One went for a rhyme;
  The other would chime,
When he found the beer bad, "'Odds bodkins,' your ale is
" As rank as a *fox*-glove (verse says digitalis);
" 'Twill poison us all, and no doubt entail us
" A nameless retreat—not a treat to regale us."
Tautology blushes at Sardanapalus.

Supposing he knew not, as many do not,
The root of a verb, because he forgot;
As a rapier gets dull when laid in a scabbard,
Though once 'twould have punctured the shell of
 a crab hard,

Yet being good steel, tho' it's covered with rust,
The weapon is there, if you open the crust.

Meet with a fool with money in his purse,
Altho' his mind's not worth a "tinker's curse,"
If he's surrounded by a sponging crew,
Clap on your hat and bid them all adieu;
For if you stay the chances are you'll rue,
And have occasion to cry out "*par Dieu.*"
If any controversy should arise—
Altho' your argument may be correct,
Back'd by good sense, and offered with respect—
You'll find too late, and with displeased surprise,
Because you differ, tho' you're in the right,
Still they'll proclaim and tell you you are wrong,
To please the poor demented, brainless wight;
And what he chants they echo to his song,
Just like a lot of silly donkeys braying,
Confounding ev'ry word that you'd be saying,
And by their brutal force of lungs revealing
That where no sense is given, there's no feeling.

Old poets used to make a verse
    Upon their "loves" expatiating,
And in long lines, too, would rehearse
    Their tortures most excruciating.

    Fancy making verses now,
        Or to compose a sonnet,
"Unto my mistress' eyebrow,"
        And all the hairs upon it.

    Those days are gone by—
        It's no use to try;
The world's getting fly to new dodges
        Since gunpowder-treason;
        With common sense—reason—
All our fires are put out by "Hodges."
    There's the "Prince of the land,"
        With a "Duke" close at hand,
Who make it a source of employment;
        If your house catches fire,
        It's their greatest desire
To give you their time as enjoyment.
        Then drink we success
        To the cause they caress;

May they ne'er meet diſtreſs,
Nor their "ſhadows grow leſs!"

'Tis jolly to live and enjoy oneſelf;
'Tis jolly to do what we like with our pelf—
That is, preſuming a man is not hard up;
In that caſe 'tis uſeleſs the pocket to guard up:
But Bibo, tho' not an extravagant fellow,
Without money found it at leaſt inconvenient
When he liked to go out and make himſelf mellow,
And often wiſhed Fortune a little more lenient.
Bibo was thirſty, and, wanting ſome beer,
He felt in his pocket with ſomething like fear;
For, tho' in that pocket at times a believer,
Occaſions occurred when it proved a deceiver.
He ſought from the top to the bottom of it,
But could not find even a "threepenny bit."
With a look of diſmay and deſperate gripe,
He clutched the remains of a ſhort broken pipe;
And then with a vengeance he ſwore by St. Jago,
As if his poor back had a touch of lumbago.
  Oh! poor Bo Bibere,
   There's no relief;

You're "come to grief,"
 And in a sad state of misery;
Not even a pipe, that chief of consolers,
Admitted by all who are jolly cheek jowlers.

   Oh! sacred place, where single friars,
   By being taught to curb desires,
   And mortifying all that's evil,
   Escape the clutches of the Devil;
   When in a Salamander dress
   They have the pow'r to curse or bless,
   And ever ready for confession
   (A vital point in their profession),
   Monk or friar, whate'er their grade is,
   Are always ready for the ladies.
     Women, women! is it treason
     To ask you to explain the reason,
   And tell us why your souls appear
   Than ours to priests so much more dear?

Confession! wondrous pow'r! which first spreads
    like a veil
Of gauze, but soon becomes as hard as adamant.
Once let its subtle influence o'er the mind prevail,
And then resistance's lost for ever to recant.

Gone! hopeless! gone! the precious liberty of
    life,
Producing grief and torture to the hapless wife.

    And thou, poor husband of that wife divorced
    In all but name! Her mind, that noble part
    Which once was all thine own, is now enforced
    By one who knows the secrets of her heart
    Far better than in all thy dreams of love
    Thou hadst the capability to prove:
    Her body still is left at thy control,
    But he usurps the empire of her soul.

Pray do the nuns whose intermural lives
Deprive them of the chance of being wives,
And monks who both in solitude and single,
Ne'er with the nuns in conversation mingle?
Are those soft, tender feelings, which the heart
Can no more disannul than bid depart,
Left blank for ever by a life austere,
Denying all the outer world holds dear?
If so, 'tis strange how they can live content
Without the great enchantment Nature sent;

Immured in living tombs, thofe great farcophagi*
Confuming human flefh like Anthropophagi.

>While we're with daily cares oppreft,
>Are we to think thofe maids at reft?
>God help their fouls! I hope they're bleft,
>   And yet I cannot fee it:
>Altho' in fombre clothes they're dreft,
>And after they are all confeft,
>Their innate feelings they'd inveft
>   As Nature's laws decree it.
>"If wifhing and the crime are one,"†
>There muft be fomething wicked done
>Either by tacit thought or act:
>   What pow'r have they to help it?
>I know not how may ftand the fact,
>Or what they do to counteract,
>   Whatever we may yelp it;
>For well we know that human nature
>At certain ages muft be mature;

---

* Peculiar ftones of which coffins were anciently made, and fo called becaufe they quickly confume the flefh.

† Little's Poems.

And is it really a religious zeal
Thefe monks and friars in their confcience feel
While gazing on fuch fcenes of lovely delectation?
Or do they leave the nuns to pine with fheer vexation?

'Tis ftrange, but true, when Time, which levels all,
And nunn'ries crumble to their laft foundations,
That workmen, when they have to overhaul
Thofe ruins, find amidft their excavations
Hundreds of infants' fkeletons—each bone
A proof that nuns don't always live alone.*

---

* Foreign Convents.—" In 1829, at Charenton-fur-Seine, near Paris, I was engaged on the works of Manby and Wilfon, under Mr. Holroyd, the engineer of the works, when, time after time, large numbers of infant fkeletons were difcovered in all parts of the premifes, which I believe had been a convent of a very ftrict order of nuns. At firft we did not take much notice of the circumftance; but when the attention of Mr. Holroyd and Mr. Armftrong was called to the fingular affair, we were directed to count the remains; and from that day we counted, and placed to one fide, no lefs than 387 entire fkeletons of infants. We took no account of parts of fkeletons, which, if they had been all put together, would have far outnumbered the entire ones which were counted. I fpeak far within bounds when I fay that there were found not fewer

Some think it right to call a prieſt a "Father,"
But the paternity I would deny,
Unleſs it's meant to be a ſign or token,
"For oft a true word may in jeſt be ſpoken."
I hate hypocriſy! and I would rather
Bequeath a curſe to my own progeny,
Than they ſhould fall into the trap that's ſet
By Rome to catch them in its fatal net.

We little know the pranks of Romiſh friars,
The where, and how, they gratify deſires;
To keep them chaſte (altho' the caſe is hard),
I'd have them all like Peter Abelard.
"Truth, like the radiant ſweets of virgin-bees,"*
In the ſame ſoil admits of no degrees;
Tho' my capacity to reach the goal
Be weak, yet ſtrong's the purpoſe of my ſoul.

---

than the remains of 800 children; and there was not a ſingle bone of an adult perſon among them. The Mayor came to the premiſes, and had the bones placed in boxes, and privately buried in the cemetery; and orders were given to huſh up the affair."—*Copy from "The Daily Telegraph."*

* Struan.

Young priests and nuns just ent'ring into life,
    Pause! ere ye cross the threshold of your doom;
Nobly attempt the world's capricious strife
    Than yield your lives to misery and gloom,
Lest, taught by wicked doctrines to forego
    The laws ordained by Nature to fulfil,
You make religion but a raree-show,
    Gainful alone to those who would instil
That what they say is right, and Nature wrong,
    That you may join their foul fallacious throng.
Seductive are the meshes that are woven
    To lure the senses with their blandishment:
The splendid robes which cover something "cloven,"
    Like panoplies which few can penetrate;
With mummeries that are outlandish, sent
    As baits to tempt the victims to their fate;
The mellow'd lights, and all the gorgeous trappings,
As hollow as the faith in "spirit rappings;"
The solemn choir, where blend the dulcet strains,
To thrill the heart and melt the softest brains;
With all those scenic, masterly achievements,
Producing in our homes those sad bereavements,
And causing pangs in parents' breasts, devoid
Of daughters surreptitiously decoyed—

These are the agencies so freely given
To blind the mind and lead astray from heaven.
But in the depth, the centre of the whole
(Like that famed apple on the Dead Sea shore—
So fair without; like ashes to its core),
Instead of leading to a pious goal,
'Twould warp the heart and paralyze the soul.

Great are the symbols which our God has given
To elevate the mind—*direct* to heaven;
And men with sense feel nerveless to refute
Examples taught them by th' inferior brute.
The smallest insect that we tread on earth
Bears in it evidence of wondrous birth;
And with intricate mechanism vies
With other forms, tho' multiplied in size.
Swift on the wing the piebald swallow flies,
Rejoicing in the warmth of summer skies
(That welcome harbinger of coming spring).
Whence is the instinct? or what gift supplies
That guiding star—that inborn power—to bring
From Afric's coast the little wand'rer back,
True in its course, without a chart to track

Through weary leagues from that warm clime it leaves,
To seek its native home beneath our eaves?
Nature's the page Omnipotence displays
To court inquiry in her secret ways;
So fair a book! where revelation beams
In one eternal blaze of endless streams—
Where Science grounds her work upon the laws
Of one unerring, one Almighty cause;
And tho' we seek in diff'rent ways to show
Our gratitude for gifts that daily flow,
Dear on the record of our hearts should be
That liberality of mind, to see
That each possessing reason may enjoy
His own religion without false alloy;
But where usurping on another's right,
The whole becomes a curse—a deadly blight.
Show me the creed enlightenment can blend
Propitious in its course to reach the end:
There would I be a worshipper in heart,
Till death proclaimed the moment to depart.

I see around a poor illit'rate race,
Scarce one remove from instinct-foul disgrace;

Ask their religion, and they only say
That absolution takes their sins away.

Ablution's better than an absolution;
And "aqua pura" saves us from pollution;
Tho' 'tis not holy by a priestly blessing
To my poor mind *that* never is distressing;
But I thank Nature, who in kindness gave
So pure an element for us to lave;
Since "cleanliness is next to godliness,"
We cannot but the salient truth confess,
That he who's fond of taking a lavation
Must be upon the high road of salvation.
If we but knew that death would settle all,
The punishment of sins would ne'er appal;
Then might some vices oft the senses tempt,
Reliant on the thought "from wrong exempt."
But conscience curbs us when we would commence
Aught that would turn the scale of common sense;
And, tho' beyond the pow'r of human scope,
Our reason justifies us in the hope
Of changes yet to come—when we shall be
Called to our mother earth by death's decree.

I'm very fond of what is called digreſſing,
Although the time we take may be but brief;
It gives a man more freedom in expreſſing;
And changing ſubjects is a great relief.
But yet the theme which my "Wax-end" is bent on
You'll find he's not forgotten, but intent on.

Oh! poor benighted creatures, like a flock
Of ſheep! The wily father's laughing-ſtock!
He ne'er could thrive unleſs the Devil's hand
Propped up his throne to curſe Italia's land,
And would intrude, by his falſe "right divine,"
Upon our ſhores, becauſe we are ſupine.
Truth needs no maſk—a fact's a ſtubborn thing,
Loud may the tocſin through the country ring.
"Up, guards! and at them!" ere the upas tree
Sprouts out its leaves, to poiſon all that's free.

I've often wondered why an Oxford parſon
Will leave his creed as if accuſed of arſon;
And, after having made our Church ſo hot,
He then departs to Rome to "boil his pot."
  There muſt be certain myſteries
  Beyond the ken of outward eyes—

Some fountain, spring, or under-current,
Some deep, some underground event,
Bad at the best, and still abhorrent.
I own like others I've a predilection
To write a curse or dreadful malediction;
And Brother Ignatius,
At Bristol, good gracious!
Attempted another which seems quite audacious;
The thing is absurd and put down as fallacious,
Excepting with monks who are always rapacious.
I'd write a curse, if I'd the tools to work;
I'll name those tools—see how I make a quirk.
Had I a raw stick
Of lunar caustic
By way of a pen,
I'd do it then.
With a dip of acetic
To act as emetic,
I'd make it splenetic
And rather prophetic,
Each word should fall
"Bitter as gall."
Think of the "Inquisition,"
Once in great requisition—

The tackles
And shackles,
The gyves and the pains,
The dungeons and chains,
With all sorts of teasers
Like pliers and tweezers,
To pull out the nails.
Humanity quails,
And language half fails
To depict all the doings
When they brought frames to ruins.
Remember the " rack,"
How it made the limbs crack,
With thumb-screws and all the sad paraphernalia,
Concocted to make up the hellish regalia.
How they all felt delighted
When the faggots ignited,
And the doomed heretics
Were burnt up like bricks;
Each one called a gentile
They'd roast like a pantile,
With fire and sulphur
That made them all gulp ah!

While the ſtench of the bodies, as reeking it
    roſe,
Was the fineſt of ſcent to the Catholic noſe.
      How they glutted and boaſted
      As the poor creatures roaſted!
      When King Ferdinand *
      (The Pope his right hand)
      Thought proper and fit
      To call Holy Writ
As a juſtification and myſtical part
Of the teachings the fanatics learnt ſo by heart,
By which they deluded their ignorant ſtate,
And trembled for fear they might ſhare the ſame
    fate.
      Still, without any acid,
      I'll not become placid,
      But will "pitch ahead" rapid,
      Leaving out all the vapid;
For in thee, dear "Wax-end," I've reliance and
    hope;
I'll ſpin and enlarge thee—I'll make thee a rope.

---

* The Spaniſh Inquiſition, firſt erected by King Ferdinand and the Pope.

By-the-bye, dear " Wax-end,"
Why did we ne'er attend
To tie up the brothers they call Davenport?
If they only had us,
With their humbug and fuſs,
They would find all their ſport
Would be briefly cut ſhort;
We'd bind them ſo tightly, ſo knotty and " taut,"
That profaneneſs itſelf and aught preternat'ral
Would be ſpiritleſs, wriggling about on the lateral.

There are great ſecrets we ſhall never know,
Unleſs we graduate as prieſts, and go
To "Tiber's City," and then kiſs the toe
Of Pio—alias him they call Nono;—
But God forbid we ever ſhould do ſo,
Let's underſtand the word to mean—no! no!
If any prieſt ſhould e'er eſſay to try us,
I hope he'll find that we are not " Pope pious,"
Tho' he may ſit and bluſter bulls and thunder—
They'll end in ſmoke, like any " nine days' wonder."

We hear of strange things with the Lawns and
   the Ermines,
Tho' high their position, yet good sense determines
That a wrong cannot be a right man in the place
Concerning the welfare and laws of our race;—
A decision there may be in matters terrestrial,
But I think not in those which we call the celestial.
Dame Nature's laid down as a maxim most kind,
That each different head has a different mind;
It may be the reason so seldom we find
That two of a trade can in unity bind.

I can't understand why the Bishop of Natal,
When tried by some heads, who declare it is fatal
(As they sit in conclave and say it's quite wrong)
That a blackbird should dare to chant his own
   song.
By all that is good—by the Great Pow'r that gave
   us
A reason to think and to act for the best—
Should two or three brains claim the great right
   to save us,
And ignore all the sense that's bestowed on the
   rest?

If I were a judge on such delicate ground
(Tho' arguments trite may be eafily found),
To another man's dictum I'd ne'er be a minion,
But would let ev'ry man ftill enjoy his opinion.
Remember " Quot homines, tot fententiæ ; "
To believe not's a fpecies of magnæ dementiæ:
This fubject has bother'd the minds of all men fo ;
Yet who knows who's right in the cafe of Colenfo ?

Revere as we may do "The Thirty-nine Articles,"
Still, errors there may be, in fome of the particles ;
They are but decifions of poor frail humanity,
And thought moftly of for the fake of urbanity ;
If any fubfcribe without raifing objections
They can't complain after of any deceptions,
However in time they may form new conceptions—
As a man who attaches his name to a bill,
For good or for ill, he is bound to it ftill ;
Or when a man's fixed in a tight pair of boots,
He feels moft acutely the corn when it fhoots.

It's well to enlighten our minds with the fact
That as parfons do preach they don't always act ;

Tho' fome may be pious, there're others I think
Who are tarr'd with a different fort of a link;
From time immemorial we know it's no fin
Believing that monks fortify well within;
And every dainty this world can afford
Is fure to be found nicely fpread on their board—
Or how can it be that thofe vile flagellations,*
With penances, fafts, and all rough caftigations,
Can ever be looked at as mere delectations.
   The wear and the tear
   The body muft bear
 Requires at leaft a generous fare.
   No one can deny
   There muft be a demand,
   And then a fupply,
  From the fat of the land.
  By this it would feem
   That water-gruel
   Is not the fuel
  "To get up their fteam."
  We are led to opine

---

* Flagellants, a fraternity in the Thirteenth century, who preferred whipping to martyrdom, and held that scourging one another was the chief virtue in Chriftianity.

How happy they dine,
And drink away at the beſt of wine;
How they chuckle and laugh
As their cups they quaff,
And freely confeſs the refectory bell
To the ears of a monk's a fav'rite knell.
We very well know a flogging don't ſuit
The back of a full able-bodied recruit;
The "cat-o'-nine-tails" is a penance too ſtrong
For humanity's laws, and can't be borne long:
The monks doubtleſs uſed a more delicate thong.
Were they ever yet known to go off in a ſwoon?
As the Yankees would ſay, "or as dead as a coon?"
Yet ſuch with our ſoldiers is often the caſe—
A ſtigma—a ſlur—a fiendiſh diſgrace—
A blot on the 'ſcutcheon of England's proud face.

We left Bibo thinking
Of pipes and of drinking;
And there he ſat brewing
Of what they were doing,
And their "little game."

I forgot to mention,
Altho' my intention,
His public-houfe, "The Horfe-Shoes" by name.
Yes, that was the place where he felt fo delighted;
When unable to go, his profpects were blighted;
At leaft for that night he would feel quite benighted,
Tho' his Polly's fweet charms he never once flighted,
So happy was he on the choice he'd alighted—
So faithful and true to the vows he had plighted.
Had another propofed, he'd have felt quite affrighted;
Her love would be loft, or at leaft unrequited.

Now only to think that a paltry fhilling
Will make a man's throat quite pleafant and thrilling,
While another will pay fome pounds for a bottle
For the very fame purpofe, to tickle his throttle.

It happen'd one day,
While his wife was away,

Bibo threw down his awl
And the "laſt" that was on his knee;
He thought of his Poll,
And wonder'd where ſhe could be:
It was certainly time ſhe was home to tea;
For when he'd nothing elſe to ſup,
He'd condeſcend to take a cup.
The thirſty feeling which he had,
And wanting money, made him ſad.
He thought his wife would not refuſe }
Some caſh ſhe'd taken for the pews, }
Given to her by thoſe who'd chooſe; }
For he depended much upon her,
And truſted greatly to her honour.
Determined thus within his mind,
His wife the next thing was to find.
But the truth muſt be told,
Tho' at home very bold,
Father Roger had hinted
The laſt time they met,
He felt great regret
To ſee that he ſquinted;
It being a fact, 'twas uſeleſs to parry it;
Bibo's head was ſo queer his legs couldn't carry it.

Now, my "Wax-end," for a little more thread;
    I find I want more,
    My theme's getting sore,
And I feel to approach it with dread.

    As it was church cleaning day,
   Towards the church he took his way;
      But what Roger faid
      Came into his head:
      He'd a kind of dread;
      And didn't much care
      To be feen juft there;
So he crept moft gently into the porch,
When lo and behold! he faw—a torch!

What means a light in the church to-night?
What can it be?—has he loft his fight?
Are his fenfes gone?—his hair is upright!
      His heart is funk
      Tho' not with funk:
      Two figures he fees,
      With bended knees.
Yes; there they are, by the fide of a haffock!
One appears to be wearing a caffock;

And what to him is really aſtounding,
He fancies he ſees his own ſhoes rebounding—
The identical pair—he'd ſwear—that they were
On which he'd beſtowed ſo very much care.
Say, was it a dream? or was it a viſion?
He wondered, but couldn't achieve a deciſion.
P'rhaps at the moment his eyeſight was doubled,
A habit with which at times he was troubled;
Yet no, that could not be "the great reaſon why,"
He only came out becauſe he felt "dry;"
Beſides, the affair looked ſo lucid and nat'ral,
The circumſtance too—being two—was collat'ral.
It ſeemed to be odd, though he was not quite certain,
In confeſſion he thought there was always a curtain,
Or ſome ſort of wooden partition between them,
But in this caſe there really was nothing to ſcreen them.
There was his wife in open confeſſion,
P'rhaps rubbing off a former tranſgreſſion;
There was the Friar uſing every perſuaſion
To do what he could upon ſuch an occaſion.
By that I imply he was doing his beſt
To teach the fair ſinner the ways of the bleſt;

Her het'rodox mind he had often affailed,
But never till now had his precepts availed.

Poor Bibo, enraged while his heart forely fluttered,
Boldly entered with feelings he'd ne'er felt before,
And in accents of grief incoherently ftuttered,
"My Mary's no virgin for you to adore."
The prieft in his dignity felt the indignity
Quivering over his head if 'twere known
   That this temporal act
   Would be noted a fact,
And carry conviction with greateft malignity,
If told to his father the Pope on the throne;
And having the power of fpeech he loquacioufly
Thought he could humble the cobbler at once;
But Bibo was nettled, and felt moft pugnacioufly
That fcience which levels a fcholar or dunce.

What did he think—what did he do?
In the heat of his paffion his Mary he flew;
He'd have killed the prieft too, only he flew
   Out of the reach of his arm.
The prieft being more at home in the church,
Bibo was very foon left in the lurch,

When lo and behold! from out of the pulpit
A voice iffued forth with that Catholic charm,
  And thus it addreffed the culprit:—
" Bibo! what will you do with your wife,
" Now you have cut the 'thread' of her life?
" You're fure to be hung if it's mooted about,
" And it's always faid that 'murder will out.'
" On the Holy Church to bring fuch fcandal
   " Will never do;
" And a double crime would give a handle
   " To Pagan and Jew.
" To commit a murder on holy ground
   " Is worfe than the crime I've done;
" So take my advice and 'let us compound,'
" In the vaults below a grave fhall be found,
" We'll depofit her there quite fafe and found,
  " And the deed will be known to none.
   " But mind, if you dare
   " To breathe a word
   " Of what has occurred,
   " I moft folemnly fwear
   " I will not forbear
  " To bring you before the Mayor,
   " And will frankly declare

"This murderous affair
"That you did it there,
"Which will make all the people stare.
"You very well know
"In the vault below
"I shall then have the body to show;
"And all you can say
"Will never have sway
"Against a priest of my name.
"A cobbler to 'boot'
"Against my 'suit'
"Would be but a losing game;
"And I fairly tell you, beyond any quest'on,
"You'd not have the stump of a leg to rest on.
"So take my advice and go out of this town;
"If you stop, it's certain that 'you'll be done brown.'
"Go forth and seek another;
"Had there been but a screen,
"That sight you'd ne'er seen
"(I admit on my part it was very remiss;
"One ought to be careful in taking a kiss).
"'I must have been green'
"When I thought 'all serene;'

" But henceforth I'll act as a brother.
 " We're both in a mefs
 " All through that carefs,
" But it's no ufe to grieve for your wife;
" She's dead—it's now your ftruggle for life.
 " I've a great deal at ftake
 " ' For King George's fake '—
 (No; that's a miftake
 I ought not to make.
He meant for the fake of the Church; but then
How came fuch an error to flip from my
 pen?)—
 " Say but you'll be
 " A brother like me;
" I'll get you at once in a monaft'ry.
 " For without any joking,
 " It's really provoking
" To think your neck's in danger of choking.
 " We muft ftow you away
 " From the light of day;
 " You'll have time for ferious reflection;
 " And all I can fay—
 " You'll have time to pray,
 " Which will greatly eafe your dejection.

" I know a 'retreat'—a fav'rite haunt—
" A lovely fpot by trees o'erfhaded,
" Where you can lay, and you can chant
" ' The light of other days is faded.'
 " It's very well known
 " The Church holds her own,
" No matter the crime you've committed;
 " Go into her doors,
 " Go down on all fours,
" And your fins fhall then be remitted."

Poor Bibo felt that he was " going to pot;"
No one could fay—"Why, what a nerve he'd got."

" Difcretion is the better part
" Of valour," we are taught by heart.
 Befides, what could he better do
  Than take a prieft's advice?
 Bibo, in grief, began to rue
  The hour when he was born;
 His feelings were not very nice;
  In fact, he felt forlorn.
   That very fame night,
   Before morning's light,

Bibo decided, and took to flight;
    But where he went to
    Why nobody knew,
  Excepting Roger and Bibo too,
Tho' nothing to do with the road he took,
His name efcaped from the hangman's book;
But had he been tried they'd have made a defence
That it was not a crime " with malice prepenfe."
I believe it's a cafe the law juftifies,
If done at the moment they're caught by furprife,
The evidence ftanding before your own eyes.
No matter, he got opportune from " a fwing,"
And faved all the quibbles the lawyers might bring.

    There was great confternation
    With the whole population
When Bibo and Mrs. were miffed from the ftall;
Some thought they had taken "a moonlight fhift."
    But when it was found
    He owed not a pound—
In fact, that he was not a bankrupt at all—
They were loft to fee through the drift.

Inquiries were made
Among all the trade,
But when ev'ry one faid that nobody knew,
It was voted by all that "the thing looked blue."

The "father" did not remain long at his poſt,
He looked very ill, very much like a ghoſt;
He might have gone off to try and repair
His weak conſtitution by change of air,
But in fulneſs of time "he cocked up his toes
To the daiſies"—a fact we're led to fuppoſe,
But where? to this time there's not any one knows.
With regard to affairs, it's as well to remark
That, like a good prieſt, he kept all in the dark.

"Coroners' inqueſts" are excellent things,
Tho' not introduced in the Romiſh focieties.
When they die, do they fly upwards with wings,
And keep fecret from all any foul improprieties?
On matters like theſe they don't keep any diaries—
It faves them a great many prying inquiries.
Be that as it may,
At this time of day

Some know "what's o'clock," tho' they can't
  have a say.
But there's nought we can trace of "Roger's
  remains;"*
If we could we should not be repaid for our pains.

   Years passed away:
   An old man gray,
   The inmate of a cell,
With pious look and brow serene,
  A tale of grief could tell.
   But there were none,
   Not even one, †
  Could dream what had befell;
Tho' oft the tear-drop might be seen
  By those who watched him well.

Known by his sanctity and grace,
The poor all blessed that old man's face,
   For well they knew
   His friendship true :

---

* Not Kirke White's " Remains," nor Rogers's " Pleasures of Memory."
   † Roger defunct.

No one came there in vain to crave
The confolation that he gave.

But tho' to others he'd impart
A fympathy which gives relief,
None knew he bore within his heart
For years a fad, a bitter grief.

He was not happy. Tho' fo good to all,
Could he o'er mem'ry throw oblivion's pall?
Alas! oh, no! the vale of tears for ever
Was that fad memory which fadeth never;
Altho' to heaven in hope he turned his eyes,
He felt within the grief that never dies.
What tho' his foul feemed centred in his fmile,
His heavy heart was breaking all the while;
For he had known love's funfhine, but its ray
Was long obfcured, and forrow held its fway
For ever o'er that broken fpirit's gloom—
A fecret for himfelf and for the tomb.

And this was Bibo—this was he
 Whom now they "Father Crifpin" call;
This the good man whofe fanctity
 Had made him the beloved of all.

When the time was allotted he gave up his breath,
And calmly reclined on the bosom of death;
So well had poor Crispin atoned for the past,
Surrounded he died with blessings at last.
To all he had known he acted as friend,
And let us all hope that "peace was his end."

He scarcely had time to give up the ghost,
When Cardinals, Bishops, and all the whole host
Of clerical men, came down to inquire
What all the hulla-ba-loo was in town;
For every "Robinson, Jones, and Brown,"
      Had been heard to declare
      That the ladies so fair
      Neglected their hair,
      And were driven to despair
At the loss of so good, so holy a friar.
On such a great man they placed all their hope—
The Cardinals stated the same to the Pope—
      When, like a young skipper,
      "He pull'd up his flipper"
('Twould quite have surprised Cornelius Agrippa)
And said: "My dear boys, 'pray tip us your
    flipper;'

"The women shall have their own way.
"Without any constraint,
"I'll make him a Saint.
"What's his name, do you say?"
"Father Crispin," say they.
"Then, by my faith, as sure as I am
"Vicegerent of the King of Siam,
"'Like a son
"Of a gun,'
"I'll canon-ize him without more delay.
"Master Secretary,
"Mind this, d'ye see,
"And enter his name in the 'Book of Fate;'
"Thereto attach our 'great seal of state.'
"Be careful, and mind you 'make no mistake;'
"Or should it be so,
"By my blessed toe
"You will probably go
"To the cellar below."

I wish to observe, to save further trouble,
In the "Lives of the Saints"* they make Crispin
    double;

---

* Butler's "Lives of the Saints," vol. x.

They write of a Crispin and also Crispinian—
An insult as great as to call him a "Fenian."

> But mine's the legitimate Crispin
> (My author I cannot refuse);
> He was known to be always lisping
> When drunk at the "Jolly Horse-Shoes."

On the twenty-fifth day of October,
A day when few cobblers are sober,
> At that time of year
> When they brew the best beer,
The name of "Saint Crispin," our Saint will appear;
An almanack get and look at the date—
I know I'm correct in what I relate—
In characters red,* the colour of blood,
You'll be able to see it "as clear as mud."

And now, my "Wax-end," I've run out thy thread.
Had our patron the Saint been alive and not dead,

---

* Saints days are printed in red ink.

There is not a doubt, without any ado,
He'd have made more of you—in mending a shoe:
With your kind assistance these lines I've run
  through;
With my very best thanks, I bid you adieu.

Moral.

Pray don't, like Bibere, give way to guzzling,
And always take the greatest care of muslin:
That both can prove ungrateful you may find,
And overturn the balance of your mind;
"Stick to your last," or any other labour,
And don't be always chatting with your neighbour.
Place not implicit faith in one another,
Nor fancy ev'ry man to be a brother;
Talk with a parrot rather than a parasite,
For one can harm you though they both can bite;
Be courteous unto all, yet not confide
In any one until their worth you've tried;
But having found a true and honest friend,
Welcome that friendship as a great God-send;
Make home your comfort, and your wife's sweet
  charms
The spell which ev'ry guilty thought disarms;

Conciliate each other with a mutual feeling—
No fecret thoughts within your heart concealing;
"For as you make your bed, fo you muft lie,"
Until the time arrives when you muft die.

Addenda.

Young wives, don't think too much about con-
    feffing;
And hufbands, ope your eyes to priefts digreffing;
Be careful, priefts, how you beftow your bleffing,
And don't be fhocking us with vile tranfgreffing.

WAIFS.

A LEGEND OF THE SEA.

II

WAIFS.

A LEGEND OF THE SEA.

'ER the enamell'd furface of the deep,
    Refulgent—like a bride upon her bed,
    So calm, fo lovely in her midnight fleep—
Not e'en a cyprefs drooping o'er the dead
Could throw a fhade upon their hallow'd reſt
Like clouds reflected on her azure breaſt.

Before that picture of ethereal light
Two beings sat, rapt in their hearts' delight;
Their hands were lock'd together, and their looks,
More eloquent than nature's faireſt books,
Were bent upon each other, while their eyes
Told joys which mortals feldom realize.

Yet met they not clandeftinely, for they
Had knelt in homage at the holy fhrine,
Which fanctified their love by pow'r divine;
And in their feelings bleffed the happy day
That gave a folace to each other's heart—
In joy to live, in agony to part.

Their thoughts were far beyond that liquid light
Which fpread before them from their homely
    ftrand;
For time had fped, and this the only night
Before they left their dear, their native land.
Ah! who but they who've found the time arrive,
Can feel how hard, how fad it is to ftrive
Againft the yearning paffion for a home,
When forced to leave, o'er other lands to roam!
How all the little trifles of our youth
Come burfting forth, arrayed with ardent truth;
How kindred all which bind our hearts to earth
Seem magnified into a fecond birth,
And reminifcences of bygone years
Add but a gloom unto our prefent fears;
Yet memory can bear to lands away
The retrofpect of many a happy day.

Buoyant the bed where rests the weary gull,
Lull'd by the undulation of the sea;
And in tranquillity there lies a hull
Riding at anchor, but 'twill soon be free;
For at the first approach of coming day
Her sails will be unfurl'd to leave the bay.

All partings o'er—each fond, each vain regret:
Yet scenes in life we never can forget—
The vessel speeds upon her destined course,
Sev'ring true hearts with feelings like remorse.
Dim fades the land: ere yet the setting sun
Throws one faint gleam, the happy vision's gone.

Borne on the ocean by propitious gales,
Which filled the area of her swelling sails,
The wat'ry element the vessel cleft,
As if rejoicing in her native home;
And as she bounded o'er the billows, left
Far in her wake a line of eddy'ng foam.

While circling in the air the sea-gull flies,
Watching the ship with scrutinizing eyes,

And dipping with her light wing on the main
To feed, then rising, follows on again.

To gaze, to linger, o'er the vessel's side,
To watch the coruscations of the deep—
Those million little scintillating lights—
To hear the seething, gurgling noise beside
Our pillow, ere we fall at last to sleep,
Are pastimes of the wand'rer's dreary nights.

The first few weeks were passed in musing o'er
The trials of the past, and coming change;
They'd find no greetings on a foreign shore,
But scenes which might their fondest hopes estrange.
He'd now a double task—to curb his grief,
And try to give his Gadra's mind relief.

" Sweet Gadra, emblem of my fondest thought,
" Fulfilling all which mentally I sought;
" Before I knew thee did my fancy dress
" A form like thine to crown my happiness.
" Should Fortune deign to bless my firm endeavour,
" We need not leave our native land for ever,

" But, when a few fhort years have fled, return
" To that dear home for which our wifhes yearn.
" Yet crave I not for wealth more than to give
" Thee comforts: for in thy delight I live;
" And as the light reflected multiplies,
" So do I twice thy pleafures realize."

" Dear Percy, hadſt thou not been what thou art,
" From my fond kindred I would ne'er depart;
" But 'reft of thee that home we've left behind
" Would then appear a defert to my mind,
" And I can welcome all, both joy or care,
" While I've the happinefs with thee to fhare.
" Reliant in thy love, my blifs is great;
" So that I lofe thee not, I fear no fate."

Such their communing; but before the morn
They little reck'd that all would be forlorn.
Scarce had they fought retirement in their bed
When ftrange commotions founded overhead:
They heard a fhriek, which rent the midnight air,
Mingled with fcreams of wild, of mad defpair.

He ran on deck to learn the dread event,
And found the ship a mass of living fire;
All power seemed paralyzed, and each intent
Useless to stay its ravages so dire.
The masts had caught, and every hope now gone—
His Gadra left in agony alone;
The flames sprang up—a barrier to his course,
Defying him to penetrate their force,
And by their great intensity of heat
Leaving the sea—his death or last retreat!
Oh! dreadful fate, with fire to contend;
But doubly so—the waves your only friend!

Upon a spar, in sad and mournful plight,
He floated with the current, far from sight
Of her his soul adored, whose misery
Was p'rhaps more abject than his own could be.
If she existed still, what chance, what power
Could save her life much longer than an hour?
And he could only watch the flames awhile
Consuming her upon a funeral pile;
Or when those flames had ceased 'twould only tell
The vessel sinking, and their last farewell.

Thus—thus was nature's fondest, dearest tie
Severed by one fell stroke of destiny.
Unconscious of each other's awful fate,
In bitterness too dreadful to relate
He mourns for her who ev'ry fancy fed :
She weeps for him as numbered with the dead.

Three days he drifted, when a pirate's band
Saved him from death and carried him to land ;
Yet death were scarce more cruel on the sea
Than doom'd to live for years in slavery.

Return we now to her who weeping stood
Upon the burning ship, lamenting him
As either burnt or swallow'd by the flood ;
And as she gazed until her eyes grew dim,
Beside the vessel on a crested wave
She saw an infant struggling with its grave.
Could she with apathy or coldness stand,
Nor try to snatch that supplicating hand ?
Oh, no ! maternal instinct inly grew,
For she would soon become a mother too ;
And, with the impulse, from the ship she threw

Herself: before the wave had time to close—
She clutch'd the infant, and they both arose;
While Providence, as if to bless the deed,
Granted them succour in their time of need:
A stalwart sailor grasped them yet afloat,
And drew them gently in the just lower'd boat.

A home-bound ship in the offing observed
The glaring light, which illumined the dark;
The captain and crew, with energy nerved,
Bore down to give help to the burning bark;
But ere they arrived at the scene of woe
The ill-fated bark sank fathoms below.

They hoisted signal-lights, that those who might
Have 'scaped in boats, or clung to rafts and spars,
Should know, could they but linger on till light,
A welcome 'waited them by brother tars;
And in the morning found three boats containing
All that was seen of that fine bark remaining.

They sailed about for hours, hoping still
To catch a glimpse of some yet living being;
But nought appeared their wishes to fulfil,
Tho' each one tried his greatest pow'r of seeing.

Where's Percy? where the parents of the child?
Gone, sunk for ever, in the waters wild!

And Gadra, half distracted, nursed the boy—
Left, like herself, another "waif and stray"—
And in her anguish felt a soft alloy
Whene'er she thought upon that fatal day;
Tho' once that child belonged unto another,
Now cared she for it as the fondest mother.

The ship returned unto a port not far
Removed from that she once had left behind;
But oh! what future life could e'er debar
The memory of him to her pure mind?
And shortly, to her great delight, there came
An infant girl to bless her Percy's name.

Now leave we her to seek on distant shores
Another "waif" upon life's tempest tost;
That Percy, whom his Gadra's heart deplores—
While he believes his Gadra also lost—
Living in slav'ry, scarce in human shape,
For eight long years before he could escape.

Once, while the pirate's crew were out at sea,
A vessel touched upon the barren strand;
They called for water, but what ardent glee
Did Percy feel to meet them on the sand;
And with the eloquence which grief bestows
He told them all his troubles and his woes.

Hard must the heart be that could e'er refuse
To listen to such grief, or yet withstand
The rescue of a life which none would choose;
They took him in the boat and by the hand,
The suff'rer to a colony they bore,
To breathe the air of liberty once more.

He thought he'd try to work his passage home.
Home! dreadful thought! for now his fate seem'd cast!
Far better anywhere on earth to roam
Than go where scenes would but recall the past,
The happy omens under which they started,
And mourn o'er joys that now were all departed.

He stayed, he toiled; and fortune seemed to smile
On all his doings, yet could not beguile

That innate paſſion which would ever ſeem
Like the exiſtence of a lovely dream.

One day by chance he graſped a friendly hand,
Warm with affection, from his native land—
A wand'rer like himſelf, who came to try
What wealth a foreign country could ſupply.

" Dear Percy! whence this abſence from thy friends,
" Whoſe fondeſt wiſhes ever were for thee?
" The only pray'r which on the good attends
" Was breathed by all for thy felicity;
" Why haſt thou left for years in ſilent gloom
" Thy Gadra, weeping o'er thy fancied tomb?"

" Is it to mock my poor, my broken heart
" Thou breatheſt forth a name, whoſe magic ſound
" Thrills through my boſom with a madd'ning ſmart?
" In pity ſay!—was not that loved one drown'd?
" Oh! raiſe not hopes which years have ſcarce allayed,
" Leſt my poor heart ſhould be again betrayed."

" She lives, and had two children when I left—
" Her only comfort, now of thee bereft."

" Two children, Carlos?—is she wed again?
" Oh! rack me not with such unthought-of pain."

" I would not, Percy, add one word to make
" Or cause a doubt thy fancy could create;
" Pity alone, my friend, for thy dear sake,
" Would wish to see thy griefs alleviate;
" But what I said are facts—though stern, yet true;
" If rumour's true, so true I'm telling you.
" I, like yourself, have been away for years,
" Tossed in a whirlwind both of hopes and fears;
" Nor have I seen thy Gadra, but have heard
" She had a little babe when she arrived;
" Since then she's had another, and contrived
" By industry, and what her friends conferr'd,
" To live. Nor is she wed again; your name
" She still retains; nor is one word of blame
" Cast on her; yet 'tis strange. She wore for years
" Her widow's weeds, and in herself appears

" A model of her sex; yet who can be
" The father of her youthful progeny?"

" Carlos! thy converse warps my weary brain,
" And a solution of the fact seems vain;
" To have two children of a diff'rent age
" Passes my power of sense. I did presage
" She would have one, so Gadra did proclaim;
" E'en had she twins their age would be the same;
" Or if without our knowledge she is wed
" To some one else, thinking that I am dead,
" The time appears too brief from what you've said;
" And through the lab'rinth of my tortured thoughts
" I find no answer to their vain resorts.

" Oh, Gadra! beauteous star! thou garner'd shrine
" Of my affections, I could not intwine
" One guilty thought in all my dreams of thee,
" Or ever charge thee with duplicity;
" If thou art wed, in ignorance that I live,
" Tho' death to me—still—still I could forgive.

" Soft as the air that 'wakes th' Æolian strings—
" Vibrating chords—so thy remembrance brings
" Sensations to my heart, which seem to speak
" Warm from thy balmy breath upon my cheek.
" For years when I imagined thou wert gone,
" I thought of thee amongst those stars that shone
" Upon my path, to cheer my midnight toil—
" Ideal bliss commingled with thy youth
" As thou hadst been on earth. Oh! happy dream!
" Radiant in all its purity and truth.
" Tho' thou'rt alive, I could not now despoil
" Those treasured thoughts within my heart supreme;
" And thy chaste love, dear Gadra, ne'er was cast
" But in a mould like mine, with life to last."

Oh! that the pow'r of wings could give him flight,
As on the breeze ethereally caught,
Swift as the rays that dart with morning light,
Or even pass to her as fleet as thought:
Such would his transit be to gain access
To her—his Gadra—in her loneliness.

Now bounds a bark acrofs the ocean foam,
Beneath the beauty of a fummer fky,
And bears our Percy to his long-loft home,
By all fave one forgotten, or well nigh.
Yet ftill he lives, and comes in anxious dread
To feek for her who mourns him with the dead.

And as the gallant fhip more quickly flies,
More quickly beats the wand'rer's careworn heart;
While as his native fhores to vifion rife
They're yet obfcured, for nature's tears will ftart,
As mem'ry whifpers with each liquid gem,
Had Gadra and myfelf ne'er quitted them.

The vacillating metal in the glafs
Anon doth rife and then again will fall;
So in his breaft would joy as funbeams pafs,
And then defpair o'erfhade it with its pall.
Thus Percy felt, and tho' in heart a hero,
The ftrong man's courage fell to forrow's zero.

Like "*ignis fatuus*" o'er a chafm fell,
Luring the houfelefs traveller in the night,
Who looks with gladnefs on the myftic fpell
Shining in beauty with unearthly light,

Until the flick'ring phantom falsely flies,
And depths below th' unwary victim lies.

Or like the light that burns near hidden woes,
Lit by the ruthless wrecker's cursed hand,
Which bids the storm-tost sailor seek repose;
And whilst he dreams of wife and fatherland
The vessel bilges! and death's direst throes
In gurgling waters his vain struggles close.

Now Percy stood upon the land once more,
And viewed that cottage erst of bliss the throne;
No recognition greets him as of yore,
No loved embrace or fond affection's tone.
Alas! the sepulchre were far more sweet
To him, for there his heart had ceased to beat.

The twilight wanes, and melts to starry night,
With pale wan Luna's beams upon the spot;
And there, by her own soft and silv'ry light,
Was Percy wending to his Gadra's cot.
The monkish robe and cowl—austere attire!—
Proclaim the wearer as a holy friar.

He gently knock'd at her own latticed door,
And humbly afk'd to fee that lady fair;
His prayer was granted, and one minute more
He faw his wife, and breathed the felf-fame air.
Oh, God! the ftrength it took him to control
That moment's trial of his inmoft foul!

Then Gadra fpoke—" Oh! holy father, fay
" What is thy miffion here—oh, pray impart.
" Can I do aught to cheer thy pilgrim way?
" Or art thou fent to eafe my broken heart?
" I'll help thee, father—for myfelf my tears
" And child are folace for my future years."

In accents low and falt'ring he replied—
" I afk for nothing, but would foothe thy woe.
" Why mourneft thou for one who, long fince died,
" Sleeps in the caverns of the deep below?
" But, though he lies beneath the billows wild,
" Thou haft a treafure in his ne'er feen child."

" She is my life-tie, and God in his mercy
" Sent me a comfort in my angel's face,
" And made her image of my fainted Percy,
" Whofe ev'ry lineament in her I trace.

" And this not all; for in that night of fear
" A drowning mother sank—her son is here!

" I was no mother then, but felt a joy
" In shelt'ring her poor orphan in my breast,
" And as kind heaven trusted me that boy,
" I've done a mother's duty, and feel blest.
" Scarce summers three had o'er this infant flown,
" When I adopted him as if my own."

Emotion shook th' apparent friar's frame;
In utt'rance choked, he ask'd that he might see
Those children fair; and straightway forth they came,
Young Hubert first, and then sweet Amelie;
And in that laughing rosy little elf
Percy beheld the reflex of himself.

Sweet calm now reign'd in that once troubled breast;
The Romish gabardine he tore away,
And there her loved brave Percy stood confest,
As she beheld him on that fatal day.
Disguise was useless; constancy thus tried
Was pure as spotless snow, and thus he cried:—

"Enough! my feelings I cannot subdue;
"My long-lost Gadra, welcome to my heart!
"And thou, my darling girl, and Hubert too,
"We meet this night, ah! never more to part!"
While Gadra, dove-like, flew to his embrace,
And kiss'd the tears upon his manly face.

THE BODY-SNATCHERS.

PON a cold November night
    Two body-snatchers went to
        work;
They never felt a qualm or fright
    To raise a body or to " burke."

The road led round an old churchyard,
    A steep approach upon a hill,
A six-feet wall the only guard
    Against the depredators' skill.

A drunken man who had to pass
    Close by the church to reach his home,
Had never dreamt of fear, alas!
    Or else he never would have come.

He felt he had a certain reafon
  To lean againft the wall, becaufe
His head appeared like plotting treafon;
  In fact he fcarce knew where he was.

He heard a footftep coming up
  Towards the place where he had fettled,
But having had a drop to fup
  He didn't feel his courage nettled.

He thought whoever it might be
  Would onward walk, not feeing him;
For in the dark he couldn't fee
  The cuftomer who looked fo grim.

As fate would have it, 'twas the fpot
  Selected for their operation;
The chofen body they had got
  Out of the grave by exhumation.

The man outfide looked all around,
  And whiftled to his mate within,
And faid—"Bill, all feems fafe and found."
  The other with a ghaftly grin

Cried—"He's a fat 'un; to my thinking
  "'Ten quid' he'll fetch, or I'm a duffer."
Says Joe—"All right! now in a winking
  "Pitch in the road the ſtiff old buffer."

And quickly down it came a thwack,
  Much to the countryman's ſurpriſe,
Who ſtarted up, and in a crack
  Ran off; while Joe cried, "Bleſs my eyes!"

And bellowed—"Here's a pretty bother,
  "And ſure the Devil is to pay;
"You'd better pitch us down another;
  "That 'tother fellow's cut away."

THE LOST TESTIMONIAL.

A LEGEND OF DUNDEE.

ACROSS the Tay,
    One wintry day,
   A ferry-boat was going;
Slow was its progrefs at that time—
   They did it then by rowing.*
    The frofted trees
    Told the degrees
Of cold in cryftal fparks of rime;
    And, whiftling fhrill
    O'er the fnow-capp'd hill,†
A fharp north wind was blowing.

The freightage of the ferry-boat
Confifted of an old frieze coat,

---

* A steamboat plies acrofs now—distance $2\tfrac{1}{2}$ miles.
† "The Law," 525 feet above the level of the Tay.

In which the rower was envelop'd.
The only paſſenger beſide
Was one—a form whoſe youthful pride
    The charms of womanhood develop'd;
        And in her lap
        She held a ſcrap
Of paper which was dear to her:
It was her written " charaƈter,"
Implying that the ſame would bear
The teſt of anything that's fair.

In faƈt, it was her " teſtimonial "—
The uſual ſort of ceremonial
When ſervants ſeek a ſituation,
The laſt not left from degradation.

The ſharp and nipping cold benumb'd
Her little fingers as ſhe thumb'd
The paper. Judge her great diſmay:
      The wind, ſo rough,
      With ſudden puff,
Caught and convey'd it far away.

" Oh, goodneſs gracious! let me crave
" That you'll be kind enough to ſave

"That precious paper miſtreſs gave.
"See there!—it's ſkipping o'er the wave.
"Oh, dear! oh, dear! 'tis gone again,
"And all your efforts will be vain."

The old man ſaw the maid's ſurpriſe,
And thus began to moralize :—

"No matter, laſs;
"Time's hour-glaſs
"Was never known to ſtand;
"But, like the river,
"'Twill flow for ever,
"While there's a grain of ſand!
"And tho' you've loſt
"What was almoſt
"The greateſt thing for you to boaſt,
"Yet, ere you leave,
"You ſhall retrieve
"It—by another on the coaſt."

And this he did with beſt intent;
Annex'd you'll find the document :—

" This is to certify, that I,
" The ferryman upon the Tay,
" With this girl's feelings to comply,
" Moſt ſolemnly declare that ſhe
" Did loſe her 'character' with me,
" While we were croſſing Broughty Bay."

ST. THAIS

THE FAIR PENITENT.

A LEGEND OF THEBES.

SAINT THAIS THE PENITENT.

The following abridgement from "Butler's Lives of the Saints," vol. 10,

> Will give the pith or gift,
> From which I've ground my grift.

About the middle of the fourth age there lived in Egypt a famous courtefan, named Thais; but the fentiments of grace were ftifled in her by an unbridled love of pleafure and defire of gain. Beauty, wit, and flattering loofe company brought her into the gulf, and fhe was engaged in the moft criminal and infamous habits. This unhappy, thoughtlefs finner was pofting to eternal deftruction, when Paphnutius, an holy anchorite, wept for the lofs of her foul, the fcandal of her vicious courfes being public in the whole country. At length he formed a project, or a pious ftratagem, in order to have accefs to her, that he might refcue her out of her diforders. He put off his penitential weeds, and dreffed himfelf in such a manner as to disguise his profession. Going to her house, he called for her at the door, and was introduced to her chamber. He told her he desired to converse with her in private, but wished for some more private apartment. "What is it you fear?" said Thais; "if men, no one can see us here; but if you mean God, no one can hide us from His all-piercing eye."

"What!" replied Paphnutius, "do you know there is a God?"

"Yes," said she, "and that heaven will be the portion of the good, and everlasting torments in hell for the wicked."

"Is it possible you should know these great truths and yet dare to sin in the eyes of Him who knows and will judge all things?"

Thais perceived by this stinging reproach that he was a servant of God, who came to draw her from her unhappy state of perdition. She burst into a flood of tears, filled with confusion at the sight of her crimes, and said, "Father, enjoin me what course of penance you think proper. I desire only three hours to settle my affairs, and I am ready to comply with all you shall counsel me to do."

Paphnutius appointed a place to which she should repair, and went back to his cell.

Thais got together all her jewels, magnificent furniture, rich clothes, and the rest of her ill-gotten wealth, and, making a great pile in the street, burnt it all publicly, inviting all who had made her those presents, and been the accomplice of her sins, to join her in her sacrifice and penance.

To have kept any would have been not to cut off all dangerous occafions, which might again revive her paffions, and call back former temptations. This being done, Paphnutius conducted her to a nunnery of women; there the holy man fhut her up in a cell, putting on the door a feal of lead, as if that place had been made her grave, never more to be opened.

He ordered the fifters, as long as fhe lived, to bring her every day only a little bread and water, and enjoined her never to ceafe praying.

After the fpace of three years, Paphnutius went to St. Antony to afk his advice if her penitential courfe did not feem fufficient.

St. Antony faid, "St. Paul the Simple fhould be confulted, for God delights to reveal his will to the humble."

St. Paul anfwered " that God had prepared a place in heaven for the penitent."

Paphnutius, therefore, went to her cell to releafe her.

She died fifteen days after, about the year 348.

She is honoured in the Greek menologies on the eighth October.

See her life, written by an ancient Greek author, in Rofweide, D'Andilly, Bulteau, and Villefore.

SAINT THAIS THE PENITENT.

A LEGEND OF THEBES.

I SING of her whofe beauty and whofe wit
Threw all the Theban ladies in a fit
Of fcandal, by the knowledge of her acts—
Tho' not heroic, yet hiftoric facts;
No marfhalled armies fighting on the plain
For life to ftruggle, or their rights maintain,
Led half fuch willing captives in their train.

But I muft change my metre, now too long,
And not at all adapted to my fong.

    Fair Thais was a virgin,
    And ev'rybody thought her fo,

Until ſhe went diverging
With Count Boloo, who brought her to
A ſtate of impropriety;
In faƈt he'd not deny it, he
Was fond of notoriety,
    Regardleſs as to price;
But when he felt ſatiety
He always tried variety,
    And ſtepp'd it in a trice.

Altho' my verſe is terſe,
Yet I could not rehearſe,
Were I required to do it,
How theſe young folks went through it;
Nor yet recount—without a dread
The vaſt amount—ſpent by the Count,
In ſhape of intereſt and diſcount,
In th' eleven lines you've read.

    I'm bound by no laws;
    I'll tell you the cauſe
    (Like a great many more,
    I could count by the ſcore):

I'm regardlefs of dactyl and fpondee;
>   My pentam's
>   And hexam's
>   Are like lambs
>   Without dams,
Or a maiden without any fond he.

I find fome lines too fhort, and fome too long,
Have crept into the pathway of my fong.
But profody does cramp one, and one's genius lingers;
And, *certes*, he's no poet who would count his fingers.
If you fhould have a Shakefpeare on your table,
You'll find that "looking at the feet's a fable." *

>   A poetical wit
>   Ifn't worth half a tit
> Which pops in and out of a hedge,
>   Unlefs he'd down with it,
>   If any pith in it,
> And fave us the trouble to dredge;

---

* *Othello*, Act. V., Scene 2.

For what is tranfcendent
Muft needs be refplendent,
Tho' the brighteft of things, we can fay,
Don't appear quite fo bright at mid-day;
From what I have feen
My experience has been
There's a greater delight
In a lefs hallow'd light—
The refinement of wit at midnight.

And yet fuch tricks as thefe won't do,
Altho' good folks at times get fou';
And ftrange, the longer they remain
The lefs remembrance they retain
Of all the rights they'd then maintain,
Unlefs like Burns, who'd never go,
But ftill would fing "The cock may crow."
Talking of crowing, it
Puts me in mind
While I've been going it
I've left Thais behind.

While Thais's character fuffer'd intenfely,
The young Count's went up, in a ratio immenfely.

Of luxuries fine—it's a shame they'd not hand her
"The sauce for the goose which is good for the
    gander."
The chronicles state not, so I am unable
To tell you the sauces they used upon table,
They had not in those days a Harvey, or Nichol,
Or the famous composer* of "Perry, green
    pickle,"
Nor aught on the shelves of Crosse, Blackwell,
    and Co.,
That epicure shop in the square of Soho,
Or "Worcestershire Sauce," which I think all
    must say,
Is the spiciest condiment known at this day.

    But where am I running
    With all of this funning,
Diabolical punning? I cannot maintain—
    I have lost all my brain
    In the first of my strain;
But the gauntlet is down, and I'm at it again.

---

* Smollett.

The gay Count Boloo,
Having nothing to do,
Spent his time in all sorts of frivolity;
He was always sought out
For a party or rout,
As affording the greatest of jollity.

At pic-nics, whene'er they went *à la Watteau*,
The Count would be found, as the most favour'd beau,
Reclining so sweetly on flow'rets and glebes,
'Twas quite picturesque in the purlieus of Thebes;
But yet not so safe, by the banks of a river.
While talking "soft nothings" you'd start with a shiver;
Instead of the fowl you were eating so gay,
As a vile crocodile had marked you for his prey,
Or perchance while admiring the flashes of fire,
Inspired by bright eyes causing softer desire;
While coolly reflecting how passion is fed,
A boa-constrictor is over your head
With still brighter eyes, dooming you for the dead.

From scenes of such horror when homeward you've fled
You find a big scorpion popp'd into your bed;
Or a centipede, p'rhaps, or a cobra capello—
Not over inviting to call one's bedfellow;
But custom's a habit which ev'ry one feels
The same, as 'tis said by " the skinning of eels."
While I'm painting such terrible blows to our feelings,
Old Nick's got me now, for the want of fresh dealings;
  If I'm book'd for below
  When I " cock up my toe,"
Yet the De'il take Old Nick, I must still have a go
While I've life; I'm not frightened of bogies;
No, nor any fantastical fogies;
If, like Faust, I've made over myself to the Devil,
The compact* was still that on earth he'd be civil.

  I cannot discover
  This girl's second lover,

---

* Mephistopheles: " I'll be your servant on earth, if you will be mine hereafter."

Tho' no doubt a rover,
And well up in clover.
"Clover and pelf"
The same thing itself
As bread is a loaf,
Tho' many an oaf
Would not easily stumble
On a rhyme that's so humble.

Her mind being open to new sorts of revelry,
She gave herself up to the joys of this earth,
And entered so fast into all kinds of devilry,
Like a second-born goddess* of laughter and mirth.
    Her *Soirées* were great;
    Young head and bald pate
    Came there to relate
    Their love and their fate.
    They could not liquidate
    Their ancestral estate.
When love holds the key which opens the locket,
How soon we arrive at the depth of the pocket!

---

* Voluptas.

THE PENITENT.

You may read in a work by the great poet Dante
Of visions and scenes in the regions below;
Or look at Anacreon about a Bacchante;
And then in your readings pray turn to Sappho,
  The soft, tender hearted,
  When Phaon departed;
Then dive in Propertius, with Ovid, Catullus,
And gentle Sulpicia, with naughty Tibullus.
  Such a great weight of brain
  Harping on the same strain,
 Proves "there's nothing new under the sun;"
  A hundred of years
  Like mist disappears,
Yet the same sort of business is done.
But, as they have described much more than I'm able
(Tho' much, I believe, is not true, but a fable),
Still, when you have gotten such scenes in your head
Of terrestrial affairs, you'll be much better led
To imagine what now I would wish that you knew
Took place with fair Thais and the gay Count
  Boloo.

Her houfe was a temple of choice curiofities,
Contents chiefly made up of fond reciprocities,
Such gems and fuch jewels fhe daily received
By any unconfcious 'twould not be believed;
For every rival would try to outdo
And ftep in the fhoe—of the gay Count Boloo:
They followed the game he fo coolly neglected,
And laughed in his fleeve, as might well be expected.

Like a bee or a butterfly flirting about
Among many bloffoms, he foon found one out
On whom his fpontaneous affection he'd rivet,
"As dead as a nail," or "as right as a trivet."
To the gay Count Boloo all thefe words will apply:
"While he'd one in his heart, he'd got two in his eye."
He'd rifle a kifs fo luxuriantly fweet,
And care not how often the dofe to repeat.

    When I mention a rifle
    I don't mean to trifle,

And tell you the young Count Boloo
    Was a Volunteer gay,
    For at that time of day
They had nothing of that fort to do.

Such was the ftate of the poll
When a moft pious old foul,
One Father Paphnutius by name,
Had ferioufly noticed the fhame
Which fet all the place in a flame.
He'd have felt horrified
Had the fair Thais died
In the fad ftate of fin
She was in.

    This old anchorite
One night " ftruck a light "—
    I mean by that,
    " He fmelt a rat "—
Which feem'd to illumine his heart with delight.
He'd throw off the clothing which anchorites wear;
He'd get a new fuit, and like mortal appear,
In the greateft of hope to get near—her ear.

The fair Thais
On her dais
Would not have thought that very night
That she'd receive,
Without her leave,
A visit from an anchorite.
When he solicited a room in private,
She never knew or guess'd he meant to strive at
A scene to her quite new, which we arrive at.

She said: " No one can see us here;
" But p'rhaps it's conscience that you fear.
" If so, dear Sir, without the slightest doubt,
" I have no private room will keep that out."

" What!" cried the Father, in his holy zeal,
" Amidst thy sins hast thou the power to feel
" That inward monitor? My task is blest!
" New inspirations now my heart invest.
" Oh, let me beg, let me by all entreat—
" Thy better feelings may thy worse defeat—
" That thou'lt renounce this life for evermore!
" 'Twas this alone I came here to implore;

" For there are days to come when sad and solemn
    gloom
" Will make thee feel thyself an emblem of the
    tomb.
" When beauty leaves thee—when the charms
    which now
" Have pow'r to rob another's virtuous brow
" Shall wither—when the lustre of thine eyes
" Will only glare to see how they despise
" The fleeting pleasures of the present hour—
" When irremeably they lose their power,
" And all the false temptations thou canst blend
" Will be inert to reach the wish'd-for end;
" For age, if sickness comes not with thy fate,
" Will teach thee griefs too dreadful to relate;
" And those who now caress thee in their lust
" Will turn upon thee with extreme disgust.
" Say where, amidst the world's capricious strife,
" Will pity yield thee aught to make thy life
" But as a swollen stream, which onward goes,
" Compell'd by force to struggle in its throes,
" Unconscious of its course as thou wilt be,
" 'Till flowing on the confines of Eternity?

" Oh, let me check thy fad, thy heedlefs courfe,
" And fave thee from the bittereft remorfe!
" By firm repentance, turn each fcene of care
" To all that's great, that's good, that's heavenly
    fair,
" And fnatch thee, as a victim, from Defpair."

The holy Father work'd fo on her feeling,
She felt contrition o'er her fenfes ftealing,
And faid: " The words thou'ft fpoken make me
    feel
" More than my tongue has power to reveal.
" Three hours grant me, Father, I befeech,
' Before I fly to learn the truths you teach."

The wealth fhe'd amaff'd in her vicious career,
Now her feelings were changed, as drofs would
    appear;
But in cafe a relapfe might tempt her to wander
To thoughts of the paft, or for fear fhe might
    ponder
On gifts once her idol, but now her regret,
In deftroying them all it might make her forget

Their exiftence, and with them all chance of returning
To the life fhe had led, now with piety burning.
She therefore determined the whole of the treafures
Which had compromifed her with improvident pleafures
Should be taken away that very fame day,
And demolifhed by fire in an *auto-da-fé*.

To the great market-place fhe had them conveyed,
And one on the top of another was laid,
Pile upon pile, until higher and higher
'Twould almoft outrival famed "Salifbury fpire;"
The wardrobes, rich carvings, the pictures and plate,
Her own pretty dais, where fhe erft fat in ftate,
With defigns of all forts, well worthy attention,
And all the *et cæteras* too many to mention;
'Twas a glorious "lot" for an auctioneer's lift,
Only wanting a Robins his hammer to twift,
'Twould furely have raifed fuch a quantum of grift,
Holy Church would have grabbed like a vice in her fift.

She invited Boloo
And the whole of the crew
To see her great roast instead of her stew,
Which made the spectators remarkably blue,
Excepting one—the game Boloo,
Who cried out "cock-a-doodle-doo!"
For he was given much to crowing,
And didn't care for mortal going.

When the monks had observed she'd burnt all her stock up,
Paphnutius conducted her into a "lock-up;"
Then he placed on the door an immense seal of lead,
"Leaden type" to the world that fair Thais was dead.
To the nuns he commanded precisely each day
To give her some bread and a pitcher of water,
That flesh in her thoughts should no longer have sway,
And a most "perfect cure" for fair frailty's daughter.
Three years she remained in this desolate cell,
When Paphnutius went out to Saint 'Tony to tell
That fair Thais behaved so remarkably well

He thought she might now have some
   . easement.
Saint 'Tony referred the affair to another,
One called Paul the Simple, a clerical brother,
Who perhaps did his best the hard matter to
   smother,
   And sent the next day her releasement.

But in fifteen days after the fair Thais died;
In the Grecian Menology she's sanctified;
And all I can hope is that you'll not deride
The thought that Saint Thais is p'rhaps glorified.

Addenda.

I can't find a moral laid down in the text,
   Tho' I think I've work'd up to the letter;
Fair Thais's morals were very perplex'd,
   And perchance I could not do much better
Than give you an adage both happy and quaint—
" The greater the sinner, the greater the saint."

THE MYRTLE AND LAUREL.*

A TREATISE ON GARDENING.

Set to Music by CLEMENT WHITE.

S Venus was tending her garden one day,
    Her favourite myrtle all drooping she
        spied;
Its leaflets were shrunken, and ruthless decay
    Seem'd to mark for its own poor Venus's pride.

Affrighted and trembling she ran to bold Mars
    And told her sad story. The warrior laughed—
" Why, Venus, my love, by your ocular stars,
" The poor thing is weakly and wanting a graft."

---

* The myrtle is sacred to Venus and the laurel to Mars.

His falchion he drew, and a laurel he sliced,
　　The nobleſt, the greeneſt, and brighteſt of trees,
And this to the quivering myrtle he ſpliced,
　　Which fluttered amid the ſoft Paphian breeze.

A plant ſoon appear'd of the laurel's bright hue,
　　Combining in fragrance the myrtle's ſweet air;
And ever ſince then a fond ſympathy grew
　　'Twixt the brow of the brave and the breaſt of the fair.

"SYMPATHY,"

AND

WHERE IT MAY BE FOUND.

 NEGRO parſon from a block
Held forth to his attentive flock,
And after having told them all
The penalties that ſin befall,
He then bemoaned unchriſtian feeling,
And ſaid, "The duty of each man
"Confiſted in his always healing
"Another's ſorrow when he can;"
And after all his exhortation
He thought he'd give ſome conſolation
By ſaying, "When the world's unkind,
"I'll tell you where you'll always find
"Out 'Sympathy.'" The darkies roſe
(Delighted, as you may ſuppoſe),

And cried, "Oh! Maffa, tell um where
"To find dat joy to foothe um care."
With knowing look, the worthy paftor
Said, as he twifted round his caftor,
"I'll tell you where—and it will never vary—
"You'll always find it in the 'Dictionary.'"

LETHE.*

THE MORNING THOUGHT OF A REVELLER.

F, in the vifion of expiring thought,
    There lingers all the happinefs we're
        taught,
I'd feize the chalice which appears fo fraught
    With ev'ry blifs, tho' to the dregs I fought—
If Lethe were the font from whence the ftream
Pour'd forth oblivion to fulfil the dream.

If in continual reft the foul might lie,
    By one quietus, dormant and forgiven,
'Twould foon the troubles of the world defy,
    And waft the fpirit to its kindred heaven.

---

    * A river of Hell, whofe waters the fouls of the dead drank after they had been confined for a certain fpace of time in Tartarus. It had the power of making them forget whatever they had done, feen, or heard before, as the name implies—ληθη, oblivion.—LEMPRIERE.

Then wherefore paufe to grafp the deadly bowl,
Since driblets kill the mind, where then's the foul?

'Twere furely not a greater fin to die
    By one deep draught, and quench the mortal fire,
Than that we feek a temporal fupply
    Of that which fome fo ardently defire.
Hark! Lethe cries, "Poor mortals! live ye on
A foretafte of my ftream, 'Oblivion!'"

"THE EVERLASTING GOLD PEN."

DEDICATED TO F. MORDAN.

THERE'S pleafure in a Guinea Pen,
    It gives us fuch a lift;
    No quill pluck'd from a Guinea hen
Could ever write fo fwift.
The pen's poffeffed of reafon too,
And eafily can help us through,
    Tho' we can fcarcely fpell;
For when we doubt about a word,
The pen's aware of what's occurr'd,
    And very foon can tell
    That if it hies along
With flourifh-dafh-in running-hand,
'Twill take experts to underftand
    If written right or wrong.

"The Everlasting Pen," they say,
　Will last for ever and a day;
　But what that extra day may be
　Has taxed my ingenuity.
　I've heard about the "Iron Railing"
　They advertise will always last
　For ever, and not then surpassed—
　To save the customers from wailing,
　They'll buy the iron to recast.
　So in the pen the gold's innate,
　And we may always estimate
　'Twill realize each pen-nyweight.

Moral.

And men, like pens, will all be worth
　Their value for their good alone,
　Since pen-itents can all atone;
　And there's no doubt but well it is
　That extra day's reserved on earth
　To settle all our pen-alties.

"LOVE'S PUREST STAR."

THERE is a preffure of the hand,
    Once felt, thrills thro' the throbbing heart—
A tale that heart can underftand,
    Tho' trembling lips dare not impart.
The hand which thus has fondly preft
Conveys the fpell from breaft to breaft.

There is a look which, once exchanged,
    Says more than e'en the tongue can name;
And, tho' to others ever changed,
    That look to thee is ftill the fame;
It tells, tho' hope delufive prove,
The heart may yet in filence love.

'Tis not that gaze so often fix'd
    When thousand lustres glad the eye;
'Tis mild, and soft, and strangely mix'd
    With blighted hope and vacancy;
Whilst thro' the film is seen afar,
By thee alone, "Love's purest Star."

"MEAT versus FISH."

A CANONICAL DISTINCTION.

A PRIEST had once a ferving-man
    Defcended from an African—
    A woolly-headed fort of nigger,
Who, tho' in conduct calm and mute,
In appetite was always eager,
    Which made his intellect acute.

The Prieft a ftrict injunction gave
That, as his precious foul he'd save,
On Fridays he muft never eat
The fmalleft particle of " meat ; "
But, juft to gratify his wifh,
He might indulge in eggs or " fifh."

"MEAT *versus* FISH."

One day the Prieſt's olfactory nerve
Suggeſted James was going to ſwerve
From Friday's abſtinence, for he
Smelt onions moſt delicioufly,
   Which James was frying in a pan;
And that his nofe—ſhould not impofe,
Abruptly from his seat he rofe,
   And quickly to the kitchen ran,
Where, horror-ſtruck, he ſtood and briſtled
To see beefſteak and onions frizzled;
   And, as the curſed feaſt he eyed,
   With rage indignantly he cried:—
" You varlet! this vile dereliction
" From what the holy Pope is teaching
" Deferves fome dreadful malediction!
" And, after all my pious preaching,
" To catch you eating 'meat' to-day
" Surpaſſes all I've pow'r to fay."

   By all that's holy blacky fwore
   His mind felt eafy on that fcore,
   And faid—" As certain as my name's
" No longer Sambo, but is James,

"MEAT *versus* FISH."

"That bit of steak is no more 'meat'
"Than sugar-cane, however sweet.
"With water you did sprinkle me,
"And said I henceforth James should be,
"Tho' Sambo then had been my name.
"Now with that steak I did the same;
"I sprinkled it upon the dish,
"And said, henceforth your name is 'fish.'"

"RECONCILIATION."

THE BLACKSMITH'S WIFE'S REPLY.

Set to Music by CLEMENT WHITE.

YOU may think as you like, but I truly can say
    That affection binds faſt where it takes;
Tho' you may not lay by for the great "rainy day,"
    Yet the outcaſt in life often makes
The fondeſt devotion a wife once beſtow'd
Still gleam on through all as it ardently glow'd.

There's a warmth in the heart that's more fervent to me
    Than the embers which warm your poor hands;
For the words you have ſpoken I've treaſured with glee,
    And my breaſt with its pleaſure expands.

"RECONCILIATION."

Oh, ever through life may you ſeek to attain
That ſolace at home which can ſoothe ev'ry pain!

Then the poor ſmould'ring embers would blaze
    forth ſo bright,
  As together we fann'd the warm fire,
And the ſparks would engender a flame of delight,
  If we'd only the pow'r to inſpire
That ſympathy left, which, united, would ſhine
In rays whoſe pure beams would be pleaſure divine.

The forge and the bellows you long have rejected
  May blow a loud blaſt as before,
And your wife, when ſhe finds ſhe's no longer
    neglected,
  Would rejoice in the old welcome roar,
As the ſparks from your anvil would brilliantly fly,
Reſtoring the comforts you uſed to ſupply.

THE WIT AND THE HOST.

A TALE OF THE LEDGER.

THE WIT AND THE HOST.

A TALE OF THE LEDGER.

ONE of thofe happy jovial boys,
   In whofe fociety we pafs
Brief hours of terreftrial joys,
   Was form'd by nature to furpafs
The av'rage of the witty clafs,
And give new zeft to ev'ry glafs.

Although his eloquence could flow,
   Yet 'twas to him no fource of money;
For, by example, well we know
   The bee which makes the fweeteft honey
May in delufive hope fly fartheft,
And yet not reap the richeft harveft.

So wit sometimes, with extra spark,
    May not achieve the point it meant,
But rather overshoot the mark,
    Tho' utter'd with a good intent;
For 'tis not ev'ry one that can
Brook satire from another man.

The landlord of the hostelry
    Was quite incapable to take
The sallies of his revelry,
    And also made a great mistake
In tendering a long old score
For grogs the wit had drunk of yore.

This rupture made the wit betake
    Himself unto a rendezvous,
Where, for his talents and his sake,
    The others follow'd (*entre nous*);
So that the former house was left
Entirely of guests bereft.

The same diversions as before,
    Of course, took place in their new quarter;
The wit commenced another score
    For sundry drops of gin and water;

While all the time old Boniface
Wifh'd that he would his fteps retrace.

He foon found out his foolifh error,
 For in the future he forefaw
That dread of dreads—to all a terror—
 The broker knocking at his door.
Poor man! he gladly would atone,
Tho' all he did was curfe and groan.

Continual thinking clears the mind,
 And, after all, he wifely thought
He'd not be harfh, but would be kind,
 For dearly he'd experience bought,
And daily sought an opportunity
To win the wit to his community.

The time momentous came at laft;
 He faw him walking up the ftreet,
And, juft before the door he paff'd,
 He welcomed him with friendly greet.
" Good day, dear fir! the weather's fine;
 "This moment I'm about to dine,

" And shall be happy if you feel
　" Inclined within my house to walk.
" My joy I scarcely can reveal;
　" Step in, we'll have a friendly talk,
" And o'er a glass of sparkling wine
" We'll speak about the auld lang syne."

And, nothing loth, the wit accepted
　　The hospitality he proffer'd;
His stomach would have much objected
　　To lose a treat so kindly offer'd,
Since fortune smiled not every day
In such a pleasant sort of way.

The dinner o'er, the host proceeded
　　Towards a cupboard, whence he took
A register of bills he needed—
　　In fact, it was the pond'rous book
In which the wit's long score was noted,
The same the landlord once had quoted.

Then in his hand he took plumbago,
　　And thus addressed his friend the wit:
" I swear by all! by great Saint Jago!
　" That half this score which I have writ

" I'll cancel through—if you'll be true
" And bid the other houfe adieu."

" What!" faid the wit, " one half the fcore off!
   " Such gen'rous conduct melts my foul."
  Then quick the other half he tore off,
    And cried—" We balance on the whole;
" From this fame day I'll make amends,
" And ever after we'll be friends."

" I'm of an independent mind,
  " And when I meet a noble heart
" Congenial with it, you will find
  " An equal feeling I'll impart;
" For I am not to be outdone
" In gen'rous deeds by any one."

  Within a week the houfe again
    Began to flourifh as before;
  The landlord knew 'twas all in vain
    To charge the wit another fcore.
  Their friendfhip met no further mar,
  For wit and wine were on a par.

THE NOISY DEBATE.

How often we meet with men possessed of a certain temperament of mind, who, having been engaged all day in the harassing transactions of business, resort of an evening to their taverns for the sake of conviviality, and, having spent the time in general conversation, from some cause or another enter into arguments which they are quite incapable of carrying out; while a shrewd man, watching his opportunity, and having gleaned their best thoughts, with a dash and daring will carry off the palm.

FULL many toasts they will propose,
    And many glorious healths they'll drink,
Till some are getting quite jocose,
While others in oblivion sink.

A man possessed of common sense
Can steer through any argument
(When two or three at once are talking);
Rise on your legs and thus comment:

"You spoke in an imperfect tense"—
Say anything by way of balking—
The Chairman then will rise to order,
And throw their brains in more disorder;
The Vice will also ask the wherefore,
While you assert your why and therefore,
Then with politeness take your seat;
But mind one thing, pray don't neglect
To bow with ev'ry due respect
Both to the Chair and Vice—the feat
Is half accomplished; then condense
The best of what each one has said,
And store it well within your head.
With seeming diffidence arise,
As if again you would commence,
And when the Chair "attention" cries
The cream of their own thoughts relate,
As if it sprang from your own pate;
It's sure to bear an extra gloss
When cleared from all its former dross:
Mind and deliver it concisely,
Declare they are your thoughts precisely.
The argument is then the bone,
Contention yields to you alone;

THE NOISY DEBATE.

And when they ſeek for a deciſion
On points of which they've loſt all trace,
Then look them firmly in the face,
And ſay it was your own preciſion
Which led them from a great deluſion—
Take odds they'll come to your concluſion.

UNTOLD LOVE.

IN IMITATION OF COLERIDGE'S "GENEVIEVE."

SHE doth not reck, she cannot dream,
    And chance 'twould not e'en pity move,
How one whom she hath little known
    Is dying of her love.

Oh, mem'ry! can I e'er forget
That moment when in beauty bright
She rose upon the purple eve
    A miracle of light?

As rosy clouds o'er Grecian sky,
Which through the liquid ether chase,
So blushes flitted o'er and o'er
    The beauty of her face;

While through the foliage of her hair,
Clust'ring around that marble neck,
Those blushes stealing from her cheek,
    Anon its snow would deck.

That wondrous beauty with a grace—
A stately virgin grace—she wore,
Which whisper'd her as one less form'd
    To love than to adore.

Her charms, so dream-like, seized my soul,
Yet, oh! 'twas fill'd with mournful fears;
For well I knew a wayward fate
    Might call me forth for years.

Yet all, alas! to me is vain,
And time itself can only prove
How twined she is around my heart,
    Now dying of her love.

RUTH.

THE GLEANER.

WHEN Ruth went forth to glean in Boaz'
    land,
    The widow's charms to him appear'd
so sweet,
That, by Naomi's wishes and command,
    She slept that night beside the rich man's feet.

Reckless of him who melted at her tears,
    And gazed with pity on her state forlorn,
The ingrate vixen pull'd his lengthy "ears,"
    And *Ruth*lessly she trod upon his "corn."

"THE STEPPING-STONES."

A RIVER SCENE.

"THE STEPPING-STONES."

A RIVER SCENE.

IN Scotland, where the laſſes wander
   O'er heath and thro' the moſſy dells,
  And by the ſtreamlets that meander
   Amidſt ſweet banks of aſphodels,
There Nature was in beauty thruſting
   Forth the bloſſoms on each tree,
And all the germs of plants were burſting
   Into new nativity.
The lark ſang ſweetly upward flying,
   And ſwallows ſkimm'd the ſilent lake,
Whoſe ſurface look'd ſo ſmooth and bright,
Unbroken, like a ſheet of light,
Excepting where the ſportive trout
The circling eddies plaſh'd about;

Or where the fwan, with ftately gait,
His feath'ry pinions beautifying
   As pure and white as fnowy flake,
With crefted neck and puff'd-up plume
Caft far afide the liquid fpume,
   And fondly fwam towards his mate.
Whilft herds in calm repofe were lying
   Beneath the fhelter of the brake.
The balmy air, with odours fraught,
The fcents of various flow'rs brought,
And wafted round their rich perfume.

The bee humm'd forth his joyous tone;
   The bufy ants were in commotion;
   While fpiders fpun their magic webs,
And in the placid fcene was fhown,
   By all things in their day's devotion,
   The courfe of Nature never ebbs.

Acrofs a ftream whofe graffy ridge
Has never yet been fpann'd by bridge,
But where the " Stepping-ftones " were placed
By thofe whofe fteps had often traced

From bank to bank the limpid ſtream—
There, on thoſe " ſtones," one ſunny day,
I met a nymph about midway
    Whoſe beauty haunts me like a dream.

One " ſtone " abruptly roſe, on which
    Two at a time could ſcarcely ſtand—
The foot-hold was a little niche—
And at a glance I could perceive
'Twas doubtful if ſhe could achieve
    To ſtep acroſs without my hand,
Which, with a bluſh and downcaſt look,
The lovely, baſhful maiden took.

Oh, what a tremulous ſenſation
    Thrill'd through my boſom as I felt,
In that brief moment's ſweet pulſation
    Of hands, what happineſs there dwelt!

I could but turn my gaze aſide
From charms ſo beauteouſly allied;
For, as ſhe ſtood upon the " ſtone,"
A hallow'd light around her ſhone;
And in the cryſtal ſtream I ſpied,

Reveal'd in Nature's looking-glafs,
The reflex of that lovely lafs—
A lafs moft beauteous to behold,
One caft in Nature's lovelieft mould;
For on this earth we feldom find
Such virtue and fuch grace combined.
A rofeate bloom her cheeks o'erfpread
As furtively, with half-turn'd head,
Her eyes, of fweet cerulean blue,
She partly ope'd, and then withdrew;
Such dazzling orbs of beauty bright
Seem'd o'er her face the tint to dight.
Soon was the tender truth reveal'd—
A truth which could not be conceal'd—
That love was twining round my heart,
And would its tender tale impart.

If young Narciffus * ftood amazed
   When he beheld in glaffy water
The aqueous form on which he gazed,

---

* A beautiful youth, who faw his image reflected in a fountain, and became enamoured of it, thinking it to be the nymph of the place. His fruitlefs attempts to approach this admired object fo provoked him that he grew defperate, and killed

Nor knew that image was himself—
  Had he but seen that fairy daughter
As I beheld her in the brook
Reflected like a mountain sylph,
So bright a picture of delight
Painted by Heaven's ethereal light,
As fed my fond enraptured sight,
He would have felt the spell's resplendence
So lovely in its great transcendence,
That, with surprise and pensive look,
  Instead of pining lone and single,
He would have wooed her virgin charms,
To nestle in his youthful arms,
And own'd, combined, they had the pow'r
  With ecstasy to intermingle,
And form on earth " a double flower."

That lassie's wed, and happy now,
  Tho' years have fled, and age has planted
Some furrows on the matron's brow;
  And e'en her hair, it must be granted,

---

himself   His blood was changed into a flower, which still bears his name. The nymphs raised a funeral pile to burn his body, according to Ovid, but they found nothing but a beautiful flower.

Which once in rich luxuriance grew,
Has now attain'd a silv'ry hue;
Yet, through the vista of the past,
  The vision of that happy day
On mem'ry's page will ever last,
  When Nature, in her grand array,
O'er hill and dale had blossoms strown,
And we stood on the " Stepping-stone."

THE DEVIL OUTWITTED.

TWO Lawyers who had always shown
    Contention over ev'ry bone
    That in the kennel of the law
Fell under their rapacious jaw,
And spiteful, as with adders' teeth,
    And very waspish in their heart,
Kept all their poison in its sheath,
Determined for a deadly bite,
    If either one should dare impart
A "*casus belli*" for a fight.

    "At daggers drawn,"
      They had forsworn

All friendly intercourſe;
And having paſſ'd life's gayeſt time
In ev'ry ſort of ſin and crime,
   They ſtill felt no remorſe;
When in the courſe of Nature's laws
Grim Death ſtepp'd in and aſk'd the cauſe
Why lives they'd led ſo curſed evil
Should not be teſted by the Devil?

The Lawyers, like "Kilkenny cats"
   (When hanging o'er the line),
Were plucky as two barn-door rats,
   Or quilly porcupine,
And, nothing daunted, coincided
To do whatever Death decided.

But when the Devil ſaw his clients,
He ponder'd ſorely in his mind,
   And felt how vain was all his ſcience
Againſt ſuch villains of their kind;
For he knew well—he could not find,
   Not e'en in Hell,
   Where demons dwell,

One to excel
Thofe Lawyers fell;
They were fo bad 'twould be a sin
Beneath Hell's roof to let them in;
Their lofs he thought he'd not deplore,
And very wifely clofed the door,
For much he fear'd each fiendifh elf
Might "turn the tables" on himfelf.

OLLA PODRIDA;

OR,

RAILWAY JOTTINGS.

OLLA PODRIDA;

OR,

RAILWAY JOTTINGS.

ONE hour to stop before the train departs;
    But then, the porter says it never starts
    Precisely to its time, but rather o'er,
Because another train must come before;
And that, he says, invariably is late;
So there's no telling what's the time to wait.
But wait I must, with feelings of compunction;
It's always so—when at a railway junction.

Talking of junctions, that famed one at Clapham
    Appears to all who happen to be foreign
As if 'twere made expressly to entrap 'em
    With ins and outs, just like a rabbit-warren.
Even the porters seem as if abhorring
So many questions, and not make a florin.

There you muſt burrow, with a kind of dread,
    To ſee which ſtairs will prove for you effective,
And very often find yourſelf Miſs-led
    By ſtockings white, advancing in perſpective:
Subſtantial proofs, ere you can reach the landing,
That Engliſh women have good underſtanding.

Now, how to paſs the time?—why, that's the thing!
It's not the place to ſmoke, nor yet to ſing.
I'm not inclined to walk, and that Havannah
(Which, coſting ſixpence, ſhould be ſweet as manna)
Was horrid ſtuff; my lips are parch'd and sear,
Which certainly entails ſome "bitter beer."

It's ſtrange there's no dependence on cigars;
As far as I'm concern'd, it oft debars
Their uſe. Give me the pure Virginian weed
Cut into ſhreds, and with a pipe I need
No greater boon; in that I feel reliance:
I'll keep to pipes, and bid cigars defiance.

What's to be done? I've paper, pen, and ink;
Now for a ſubject, and the brain to think!

Oh, sunny Thought! come whisper in my ears,
That I may book thee; for my pen appears
As if a dip of ink would do it good:
'Tis a sad glutton, and it never would
Be quiet for a moment, but keep scribbling
As sure as mouse at toasted cheese keeps nibbling.

Now, dearest Psyche!—emblem of the soul!—
Give me the thought—the pen's at thy control!
Oh, elevate me with thy wings to try
The realms of space, like thee, bright butterfly!
What! deaf to my entreaty?—no reply?
Thou know'st I cannot grasp thee, so good-bye!

Delve then, my Muse, into funereal urn,
   Promethean like, and filch the latent fire,
If smould'ring in the grave it yet can burn;
   For thou wouldst then be able to inspire
Me with a theme from regions drear and dread,
To teach the living secrets from the dead.

Now dive into the density so deep
Of oceans wide, and see if thou art able
To gain th' immortal prize that we should reap,
Couldst thou but clutch the "great Atlantic Cable."

There sleeps the spark, although it dormant lies,
Like urn in earth, embedded in the sand;
Yet, like the Phœnix, 'twill again arise
To stretch from shore to shore the firebrand.

   And thou, Pandora—
   The greatest bore a
   Man ever knew
   With cause to rue—
Say, what could be thy vicious scope,
  With thy infernal "Box of Pills,"
  Scattering about all sorts of ills :
 Then say—there's nothing left but
   "Hope ?"

Goddess of Chastity! thou fair Diana!
What marvels to thy lustrous name belong;
'Twere better to invoke thee on piano,
For I could not in purity of song
Sing of thy midnight trip into the cave
Where young Endymion lay so fast asleep.
Say, didst thou only go to take a peep?
Or from what cause didst thou so misbehave?

Thou surely must have been a lunatic
Ever to think of playing such a trick.
What were those feelings which could act ye on,
When once upon a time poor Actæon,
Who only, like thyself, did take a peep,
But ever after had dire cause to weep.
How was a man, while hunting, to suppose
He'd catch a lady without bathing-clothes;
And then the deed thou didst was nought to brag,
To turn so fine a youth into a "Stag;"
No wonder madmen suffer from the moon, a
Word synonymous with thine, " Chaste Luna."

   There's a face in the moon,
    And there's one in a spoon,
  If you doubt you had better see in it;
   And another is found
    On a tea-pot that's round,
  But mind it's not hot with tea in it.
The spoony one looks very much elongated;
The other is jolly, like "Spurgeon," elated;
It's strange that such trifles should seem so complex,
 But there're always two sides to a picture;
Some like the concave, and some the convex;
 Take your choice, I won't raise any stricture.

Hail! Venus! Goddefs of the Cyprian Ifle!
Come forth in all thy beauty, with a fmile
Of welcome; for a vot'ry of thine own,
Oft have I been a fuppliant at thy throne.
Give me a theme that tender hearts may touch.
What! filent ftill? then p'rhaps I afked too much.

I've fought the goddeffes—and yet it feems
As well to "go to Bath"—to get my themes;
Since in Elyfium I'm denied a berth,
I needs muft grovel on my mother earth,
And feel fome confolation in the fact,
Since heathen ladies don't know how to act;
   And if ideal
  Subjects can't be found,
   I'll keep to real.
  Now a glance around—
"From the ridiculous to the fublime"
I've tried; now trot, my Mufe, in humble rhyme.

There are three ladies of the maiden type,
Whofe fummer bloom is rather more than ripe,
And in their ftyle they certainly appear
As if they moved in a fuperior fphere;

But very angry ſeems their warm debate,
I wonder what it is that they relate?
What can have put them in ſo hot a ſtate?
Yet one thing's certain, which I can deſcry,
That beauty's not enhanced when words run high.
'Tis ſtrange three women cannot live together
Without a quarrel, or a quibble—whether
The day will turn out fine, or rainy weather,
Or ſome ſuch trivial thing as men would bluſh at,
A point which women ſtrenuouſly ruſh at,
And all the ardour of their brain appears
To tantalize each other into tears;
But men, whene'er you ſee them fraternize,
Say "My dear boy!" as if to patronize
Each other with the kindeſt reciprocity,
Regardleſs as to age, or youth's precocity.

Men feel at times a certain elevation
Produced by wine, which women ſcorn to know,
In faƈt, they ſpurn it as a deſecration;
Tho' I have watched at times a certain glow,
Combined with other queer peculiarities,
Denoting there had been familiarities

Between the bottle and themfelves conneftable;
But no, I muft be wrong, they're too refpeftable,
And wouldn't do fuch things, howe'er deleftable.

Now ftanding on the platform—there's a fight—
A flim young man, above the average height,
With legs attenuated like a fpider,
And whip in hand, though he is no horfe rider;
He feems ariftocratic in his bearing,
Yet a detefted " billy-cock " he's wearing.
With all the queftions about " who's your hatter,"
There's little tafte difplayed about the matter.
Befide the " old black hat," I fee no " tile "
But bears the ftamp of a plebeian ftyle,
Excepting that famed one of " Peter Rubens,"
The which of fhillings would about coft two tens,
  That is a fovereign I mean,
  Which bears the image of the Queen;
  And when you have the bill to fettle,
  You muft of courfe fhell out the metal.
But, tho' the fhape is good, 'tis large, and then
It would extinguifh many little men;
And hatters muft be dull, or do not care
About a fummer hat that's fit to wear.

I've done with hats. That whip's to reprimand
A little dog, which fears to fit or ſtand,
But ever keeps a leer upon the whip,
Expecting it, if he ſhould dare to trip.
Ignoble element in men to find
Brains brainleſs but to curb the canine mind.

Oh, what a noſe! 'twould make an eagle bluſh!
Oh, Wellington! (but, as he's dead, I'll huſh).
No hawk nor owl, with their moſt ſapient look,
Would ever dare to gaze on such a hook;
Yet thoſe who have a noſe which breaks the line
Derive it from the eagle—"aquiline;"
Or, turn'd the other way, and not ſo ſnug,
From dog (almoſt extinct) they call "a pug."
Give me the noſe that's neither one nor t'other,
But takes a happy medium 'twixt the two,
Such as Apollo's, and a certain few
Examples left us ſtill from Greece, their mother.

Ha! see that porter there, with ingenuity
Baffling the railway law about "gratuity!"
See how he ſtands, with finger on his lip,
Whilſt with the other hand "he takes a tip."

Well! if some gen'rous people feel inclined
To treat civility by being kind,
I see no cause why they should ever smother
The impulse—"One good turn deserves another"—
As public servants take them, great and small;
I've always met with courtliness from all.

There is a youth with Dr. Watts's hymns,
Observe his eye how busily it skims—
  Not that most moral book
  (Belonging to his little brother);
  He only holds it as a blind,
  While he directs his look
  Of modesty upon another
  Whose loveliness still brings to mind
"How fair is the rose! what a beautiful flower."
Her features disclose—a most magical power.

Upon a settle sits a Volunteer,
Who's evidently primed himself with cheer;
He has enrolled to act as our defender,
And in his feelings is a "Young Pretender;"
I mean that Charles for whom so many drew
The sword, but after all it wouldn't do.

I note a man; he's playing with a child,
But in their faces fee no fimilarity;
Is he the father? No! The lady fmiled,
And feem'd herfelf inclined for jocularity;
But I've been told fome people give a cake,
"And kifs the baby for the mother's fake."

In durance vile I fee a ftrong man ftands,
With bracelets bright encircling his hands,
  Or rather wrifts;
  See how he twifts,
While two policemen hold him in command.
  It's eafy for conftruing
  His "game" was for undoing
Some noble charter of the Britifh land.

A coffin and a racehorfe fide by fide,
A widow in her weeds, and then a bride
Fill up the vacuum of our ftrange career,
Where all things mortal unto death appear;
And yet the link which binds our lives, alas!
Totters upon the fhuntings as we pafs.

Hark! there's a sound which makes my heart rejoice.
Yes; 'tis that fame old porter's nafal voice—
"Heigh, zur! baint you for Pad-ding-ton?
Yez's beft be fharp before the train be gone."

THE BARON

AND HIS ADVISERS.

 LIMB of the law and a lamb of divinity
Once felt on a fubject the greateft affinity,
For a Baron they knew
Who'd a fine revenue,
Which at death might be left
To the folks who moft deft
Could curry the favour of fuch a rich man;
And, knowing the proverb that "life's but a fpan,"
While mutually fharing their hoft's hofpitality,
The Lawyer fummed up of his wealth the totality,
While the Parfon defcanted on death and morality.

One day, after feafting and merrily fpending
The evening in drinking, with harmony blending,

Ere they had departed, the Baron ſo bold,
From turbot and lobſter, or p'rhaps from a cold,
Fell grievouſly ill, when a meſſenger ran
To ſummon the aid of a medical man.
While the Doctor and Baron were quiet together,
The Prieſt and the Lawyer (both "birds of a feather")
Stepp'd into a room, where, as cautious as mice,
They enter'd at once into mutual advice.

The Lawyer knew well how the wealth was beſtow'd,
 Since he'd formerly drawn out the will,
And with ſad diſappointment he eaſily ſhow'd
That what had been left to himſelf and his friend
 (After all their attention), was ſtill
From the bulk of the fortune a ſmall dividend;
And calmly propoſed, if the Baron ſhould die,
As they placed in each other—the faith of a brother,
The original will they might p'rhaps falſify,
Or deſtroy it at once, and then make out another.
  Tho' the two were moſt heedful,
  Yet the Doctor was needful,

To settle the matter they then had in hand,
  And the firſt opportunity
  They sought his community,
And with overtures found him moſt pleaſant and bland.
  Then theſe three men profeſſional
  Form'd a court or confeſſional,
And againſt the bold Baron concoƈted a plot
That by poiſon that night he ſhould meet his upſhot.

The Devil was ſtrolling about on the prowl,
When a sound caught his ear like an Iriſh howl,
And he felt in his heart (if the Devil has one)
That Death was performing the part of a dun,
And he wonder'd how ſome of the Iriſh folk
Could be hood-wink'd ſo well by a prieſt's ſilly joke,
As if he'd a taliſman under his cloak ;
  And the row that they make
  At a dead Paddy's wake
    Through the ear
    Rings ſo clear
  That no one can miſtake.
But the ſound that he heard had a different cadence;
'Twas no ſcream for a ſoul, that from earth then had made hence,

For he heard not the cry,
"Ah! fure, why did ye die?"
But more like rejoicing it feem'd to imply.

The trio were chatting away in their glee,
Hob-nobbing each other in great ecftafy,
When a form diabolical, "*as in prefenti,*"
Prefented itfelf and cried out, "You all meant I
"Should be in the dark;
"But mind this remark—
"When a Lawyer, a Doctor, and then a Divine,
"Come and chuckle and crow o'er a dead perfon's wine,
"There needs not on my part fo very much fcience
"To judge there's unholinefs in the alliance.

"This man had bequeath'd all his fortune in charity,
"When you, in your greed, with the greateft barbarity
"To rob thofe in want, went and cancell'd his will,
"Making one in your favour your pockets to fill,
"And then bribed the Doctor his patient to kill."

The Lawyer admitted the will was his writing,
But infifted 'twas done by the others' inditing.

Cried the Doctor, "I own, for the fake of my meed,
"From the pangs of this world the poor finner I freed."
Said the Parfon, "I tacitly witnefs'd the deed."

"But who forged his name?" faid Old Nick, with a paufe.
"No one's done it yet," cried the Lawyer, becaufe
"Whoe'er does it beft is to gain the applaufe."
Then the Devil exclaim'd, "As I'm bound by no laws,
"I'll do it myfelf—clap the pen in my claws;
"For when you all die, as you're certain to come
"To the regions below, which will be your laft home,
"I'll leave you juft now to your pleafure and mirth,
"Since I find I'm fo well reprefented on earth."

> But the Baron fo bold
> Was not eafily "fold;"
> Tho' they thought they had "fettled his hafh,"
> He lay fnug in bed
> And heard what they faid
> About his eftates and his cafh.

By dint of good luck he had juft "faved his bacon;"
For the poifon the Doctor had fent to be taken

He pour'd in a wine-glaſs inſtead of his throttle,
And then put it ſafely again in the bottle.
Of phyſic he'd always the greateſt antipathy,
And thought to himſelf in each drop that I drip
    I fee—
Something that looks like a mixture that's nauſeous.
So he taſted one drop, as he always was cautious,
Tho' not from a doubt that 'twas poiſon within it—
He didn't ſuſpect ſuch a thing for a minute.
But inſtead of the phyſic he took *eau de vie*,
Which kept him alive to "a dead certainty;"
Yet the one drop of poiſon, by fortunate chance,
Only brought on a ſort of a torpor or trance,
    From which he awoke
    In the midſt of their joke,
And felt very ſhocked for humanity's ſake,
Tho' about "Cloven Horny" he felt no miſtake;
For, as ſlyly he caſt his eye over the counterpane,
He ſaw ſuch an object he ne'er wiſh'd to ſee again.
But he little expected the Devil that night
Would have ſhown up his friends in their colours
    ſo bright;
And wiſely determined, as ſoon as they'd fled,
Not to take any notice of what had been ſaid :

Since " Old Nick " was in league, he thought it was beſt
To keep his own counſel and let matters reſt.
    And Hiſt'ry relates
    He ſold his eſtates,
  And made up his mind that hereafter
All profeſſional men ſhould be kept at arm's length,
Since 'twas only by good luck and bodily ſtrength
  He awoke 'midſt their horrible laughter.

CLAYTON & Co., Printers, Bouverie Street, London, E.C.

www.ingramcontent.com/pod-product-compliance
Lightning Source LLC
Chambersburg PA
CBHW031817230426

43669CB00009B/1171